No-Code Oracle APEX
For
Thirteen To Ninety

Build Your First Web App without Writing a Single Line of Code

Riaz Ahmed

NO-CODE ORACLE APEX FOR THIRTEEN TO NINETY

ISBN- 9798633930535

ABOUT THIS BOOK

This book is for anyone who wants to become a web developer but is scared of writing tons of code and is looking for the easiest track to start with. I got the idea for this book from my neighbor's son who was studying computer science. Few months ago he approached me to discuss his IT project. He was very dejected and from his discussion I realized that the cause of his depression was the platform he was using to create the project, which involved lots of coding. Choosing such heavy coding platforms for absolute beginners is not a good idea - they need something very simple to get on the track. Keeping in view the scenario, I compiled this book for everyone (especially teens) to make programming fun for them rather than a nightmare.

Oracle APEX is a low-code application development framework. Low-code is a software development approach that enables the delivery of applications faster and with minimal hand-coding. Low-code framework helps you create complete applications visually with the help of drag-and-drop interface and wizards. Rather than writing thousands of lines of complex code and syntax, low-code platforms allow you to build complete applications with modern user interfaces, integrations, data and logic quickly and visually. Oracle APEX is one such area.

You can use Oracle APEX free of charge – either as part of an existing Oracle Database license or running in the free Oracle Database 18c XE product. Oracle APEX empowers you to build incredible apps and solve real problems. And you won't need to become an expert in a vast array of web technologies. Oracle APEX is capable to do the heavy lifting for you. You just need to focus on the problem to be solved.

This book is written for people of any age who have a desire to become web developer. The main objective of this book is to give you a jump-start in the exciting world of web application development and to make you a web application developer in a short time span. If you start learning to develop web apps today, you can actively perform your role in this fast-changing world. It is the skill of the 21st century. Organizations today need more problem-solving ability than ever before, and almost every career opportunity involves technology as a mandatory prerequisite. It is the only occupation that doesn't need master or doctoral degrees.

Mark Zuckerberg developed Facebook in 2004 when he was a college student. In 2014, 1.4 billion people were using Facebook every month. Facebook demonstrates the power of technology to engage billions and to reach more people. Mark just spent his time doing things that interested him and he did them obsessively because it was fun. Don't try to be someone else. Be yourself. You can't create the Big Thing right now, but you can create the few small things, and bring them up so they grow bigger. If you haven't started creating something yet, get started now! I welcome you to the exciting world of web application development. If you need any kind of assistance from me, just give me a shout via my email address - I'm always available to help you out.

URL to Download Book Source

The files used in this book can be downloaded from the following URL. On the ensuing page in your browser, ignore the message and just click the blue Download button. After downloading, use WinZip or WinRar utilities to extract the archived file.

https://tinyurl.com/ruyx75o

- Riaz Ahmed
Author
oratech@cyber.net.pk

CONTENTS

1

Jump Start to
Oracle APEX

1.1 What is Oracle APEX?

Oracle APEX is a low-code rapid application development platform that helps you develop rich interactive web apps fast. With this amazing framework you can build scalable and secure enterprise apps with world-class features that can be deployed and accessed anywhere, anytime.

ORACLE APEX A LOW-CODE PLATFORM

Oracle APEX is a low-code platform that accelerates the application development process via its built-in features. Rather than writing a heap of complex code, Oracle APEX allows you to build complete applications with modern user interfaces, integrations, data and logic visually and instantly.

DECLARATIVE DEVELOPMENT

Most of the tasks are performed with the help of built-in wizards that help you create different types of application pages. Each wizard walks you through the process of defining what you are expecting to achieve. Once you're comfortable with Oracle APEX, you can ignore the wizards and generate your applications directly.

ONE-SIZE-FITS-ALL

Applications created in Oracle APEX use Universal Theme, which enables you to build modern web applications without requiring extensive knowledge of HTML, CSS, or JavaScript. Universal Theme is an example of a responsive user interface theme in which the page layout fits the available space regardless of the device, and the same application can be viewed on a desktop computer, laptop computer, tablet, and smartphone.

1.2 APEX Applications

Applications in Oracle APEX are created via App Builder and each application comprises one or more pages that are linked together using navigation menu, buttons, or hypertext links. Usually, each page carries items, buttons, and application logic. You can show forms, reports, charts, calendars, and maps on these pages and can perform different types of calculations and validations. In this book, you will do all this declaratively using built-in wizards, without writing any code.

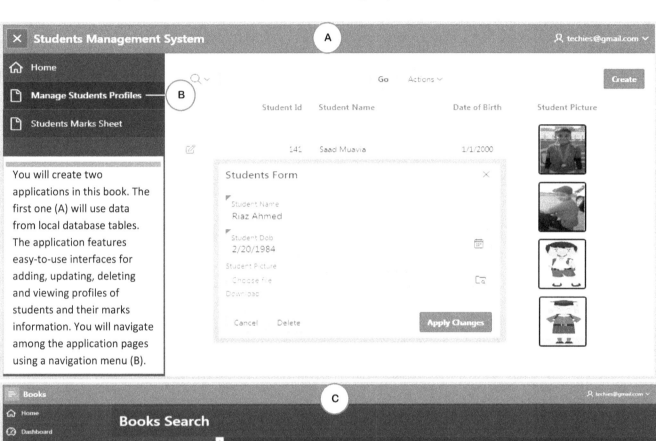

You will create two applications in this book. The first one (A) will use data from local database tables. The application features easy-to-use interfaces for adding, updating, deleting and viewing profiles of students and their marks information. You will navigate among the application pages using a navigation menu (B).

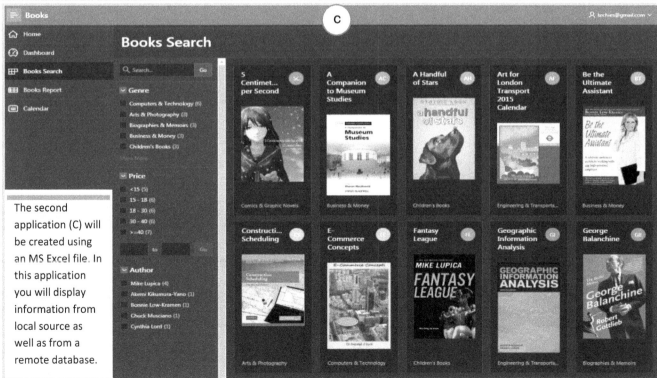

The second application (C) will be created using an MS Excel file. In this application you will display information from local source as well as from a remote database.

1.3 Anatomy of Oracle APEX

The following diagram depicts anatomy of Oracle APEX.

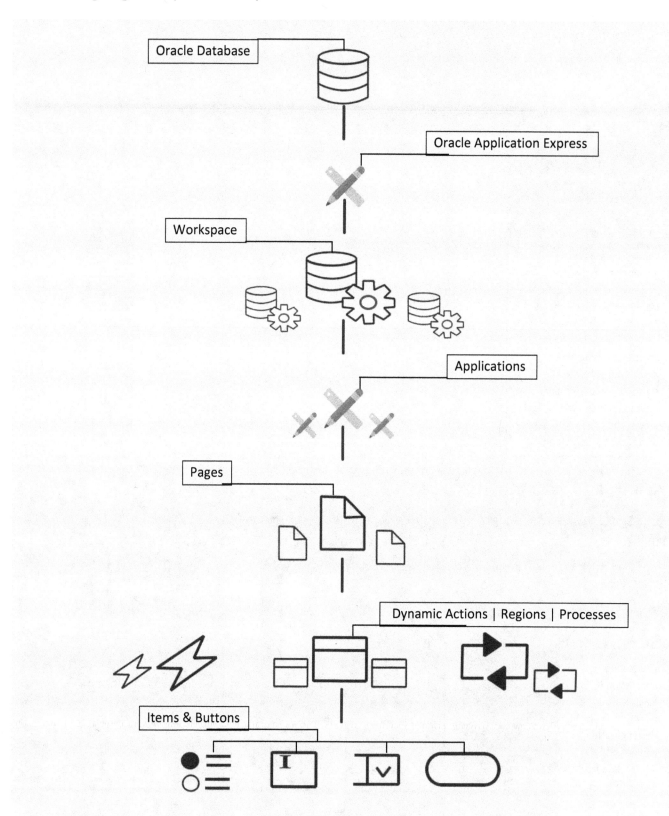

Oracle Database	Oracle Database is the industry's leading database that delivers cutting-edge innovations. The latest revolutionary Oracle Autonomous Database is self-driving, self-securing, self-repairing, and designed to eliminate error-prone manual data management.
Oracle Application Express	Oracle Application Express (Oracle APEX), is a low code web application development tool for the Oracle Database. Oracle APEX is an integral part of Oracle database. It is a free rapid application development tool that runs inside an Oracle database instance. Oracle APEX enables you to design, develop and deploy beautiful, responsive, database-driven applications, either on-premises or in the cloud. Using only a web browser and limited programming experience, you can rapidly develop and deploy professional applications that are both fast and secure for any device, from desktop to mobile. Oracle Application Express combines the qualities of a low code tool, productivity, ease of use, and flexibility with the qualities of an enterprise development tool, security, integrity, scalability, availability and built for the web.
Workspace	In Oracle APEX, you can create multiple workspaces in which you host different types of applications. To access Oracle APEX development environment, users sign in to a shared work area called a Workspace. A workspace is a virtual private container allowing multiple users to work within the same Oracle APEX installation while keeping their objects, data and applications private. You have to create a workspace before you create an application. It is necessary because you have to specify which workspace you want to connect to when you log in. Without this piece of information, you are not allowed to enter Oracle APEX.
Applications	Each workspace can also hold multiple applications. Applications in Oracle APEX are created via App Builder and each application consists of one or more pages that are linked together using navigation menu, buttons, or hypertext links. Developers use App Builder to create and manage applications and application pages. The App Builder home page displays all installed applications in the current Oracle APEX instance. When a developer selects an application to edit, the Application home page appears. Use the Application home page to create, modify, delete, run, import, or copy applications. In Oracle APEX you can create a fully functional database application based on tables, or an application that is created from a file, such as MS Excel xls file.
Pages	Database applications created in Oracle APEX comprise two or more pages. A page is the basic unit of an application. When you build an application using App Builder, you create pages containing user interface elements, such as regions, items, navigation menu, lists, buttons, and more. Each page is identified by a unique number. By default, page creation wizards automatically add controls to a page based on your selections. You can add more controls to a page after its creation by using the Page Designer interface. Usually, the Create Page wizard is used to add components such as report, chart, form, calendar, or tree to a page. In addition to creating application pages through wizards, you have the option to create a blank page and add components to it according to your own specific needs. The Application Express engine dynamically renders and processes pages based on data stored in Oracle database tables. To view a page, you request it from the Application Express engine via a URL.
Regions, Dynamic Actions, Processes	You can add one or more *regions* to a single page to display or receive data. It is an area on a page that serves as a container for content and page elements, such as items and buttons. Oracle APEX supports many different region types including Static Content, Classic Report, Interactive Report, Interactive Grid, Chart, and more. With *dynamic actions* you can define complex client-side behavior declaratively without the need for JavaScript. *Processes* are logic controls used to execute Data Manipulation Language (DML) or PL/SQL. Processes are executed after the page is submitted. A page is typically submitted when a user clicks a button.
Items & Buttons	After creating a region on a page, you add items and button to it. An item can be a Text Field, Text area, Password, Select List, Checkbox, and so on. Each item has its own specific properties that affect the display of items on a page. The name of a page item is preceded by the letter P followed by the page number – for example, P5_STUDENT_ID represents student ID item on page 5. Just like desktop applications where you place buttons on your forms to perform some actions, in web applications too, you can create buttons to submit a page or to take users to another page (redirect) within the same site or to a different site.

1.4 Request Free Workspace

To access Oracle APEX development environment, users sign in to a shared work area called a Workspace. A workspace is a virtual private container. You have to create a workspace before you create an application in Oracle APEX. For your convenience, this section will walk you through to create a free workspace on Oracle servers to execute the exercises online.

Here's a checklist to get your free workspace. These steps are visually elaborated on subsequent pages.

1. Go to https://apex.oracle.com/en/, click the Get Started for Free button. On the Get Started page, click the Request a Free Workspace button.

2. On the Identification page, enter your full name, e-mail address, and the name of the workspace you intend to create.

3. Select the options provided on the Survey page.

4. On the Justification page provide a justification for using this platform.

5. Accept agreement terms.

6. Soon after submitting the request, you'll get a confirmation e-mail from Oracle. Click the Create Workspace button in the email to complete the approval process.

7. Click the Continue to Sign In Screen button.

8. Set your password on password page.

9. You will be taken to your workspace home page.

STEP

1

Open your internet browser and type **https://apex.oracle.com/en/** in the address bar. On Oracle APEX page, click the **Get Started for Free** button (A). On the Get Started page, click the **Request a Free Workspace** button (B).

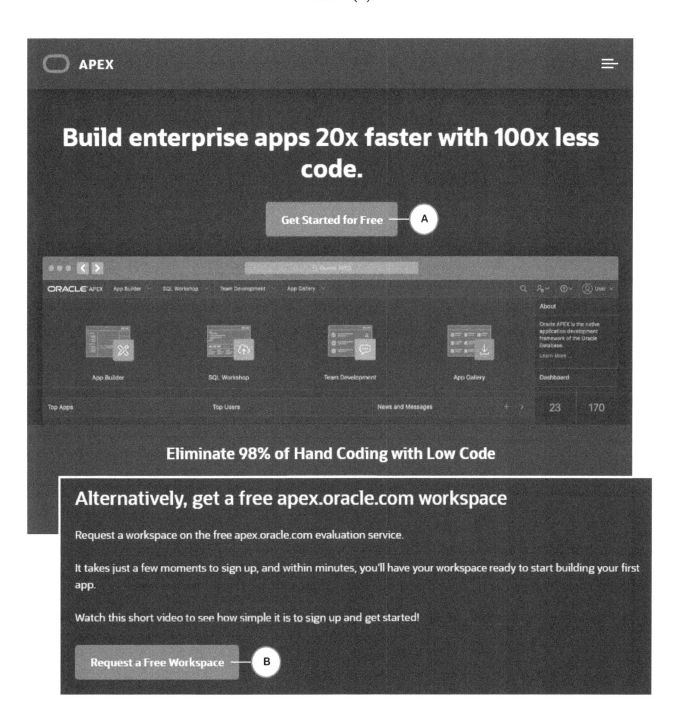

STEP

2

On the Identification wizard screen, enter your first and last names, e-mail address, and the name of the workspace you intend to create – for example, MYWS. After providing this information, click **Next** (A) to proceed to the next wizard step.

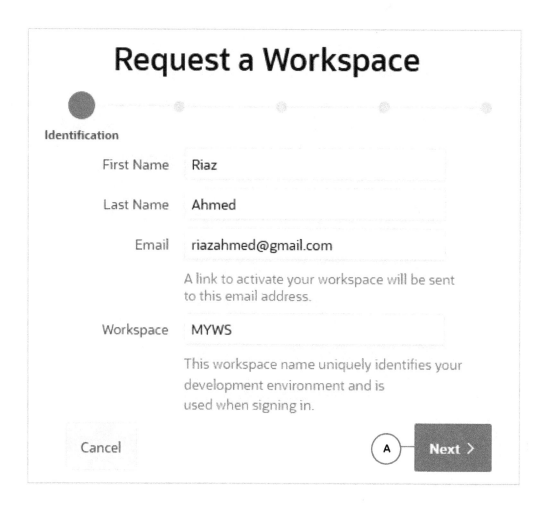

Request a Workspace

Identification

First Name	Riaz

Last Name	Ahmed

Email	riazahmed@gmail.com

A link to activate your workspace will be sent to this email address.

Workspace	MYWS

This workspace name uniquely identifies your development environment and is used when signing in.

Cancel   (A) Next >

STEP

Select the options provided on the Survey page as illustrated in the following figure, and click **Next**.

Request a Workspace

Survey

Please help us by filling out this short survey prior to signing up for a workspace. The information provided by you will be collected and used pursuant to the Oracle Privacy Policy

* Are you new to Oracle Application Express?

- ◉ Yes
- ◯ No

* Do you plan to use this workspace for a university class or training?

- ◯ Yes
- ◉ No

‹ Cancel

Next ›

STEP

4

On the Justification screen you can provide a justification like, **"I want to evaluate Oracle APEX."** Click **Next.**

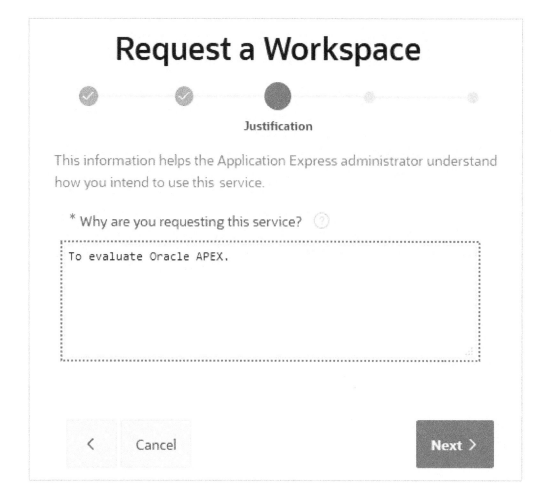

STEP

On the Agreement wizard screen, read the agreement terms and accept them by placing a check mark (A). Click **Next** to proceed to the final wizard screen.

Request a Workspace

Agreement

This information helps the Application Express administrator understand how you intend to use this service.

```
users as if they were members of the same enterprise.
You agree to respect the other participants and not
interfere with their experience. You agree that you
will not send unsolicited communication to other
participants using any Cloud Services channel (email,
instant messaging, documents, etc). You agree that you
will not send unsolicited communication to anyone
outside of the service environment with the exception
of your users.

Last updated 21 May 2018
```

 ☑ **I accept the terms** ──(A)

‹   Cancel   **Next ›**

STEP

6

Click the **Submit Request** button on the final Confirmation screen. A confirmation box will pop up with the message "You will receive an email to activate your workspace once this request has been approved."

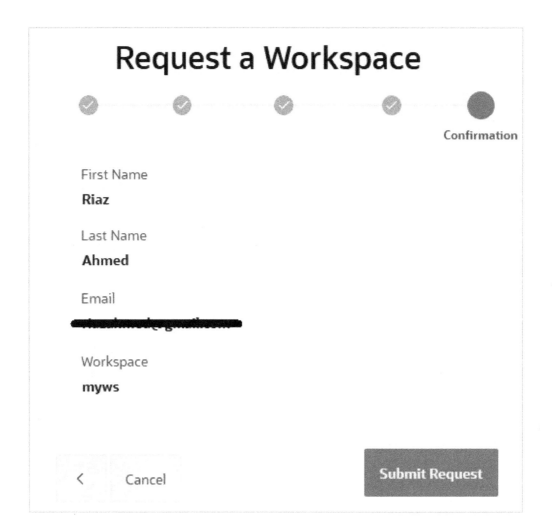

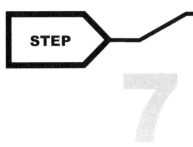

STEP

Soon after submitting the request, you'll get an e-mail from Oracle carrying your workspace credentials (A) and a button labeled Create Workspace (B). Take a note of your credentials and click this button to complete the approval process. You will be taken to Oracle APEX's website, and after a little while, your request will be approved (C) with the message "Workspace Successfully Created." Click the **Continue to Sign In Screen** button (D).

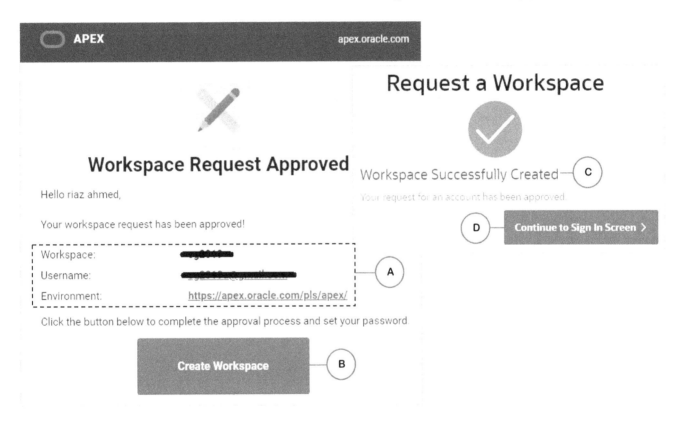

STEP

8

A screen appears requesting you to change password. Enter and confirm your password. The first text box on this screen (A) displays your username, which is your email address. Write down your password along with the credentials you noted in the previous step. You need this information whenever you attempt to access your online Oracle APEX workspace. Click the **Change Password** button (B).

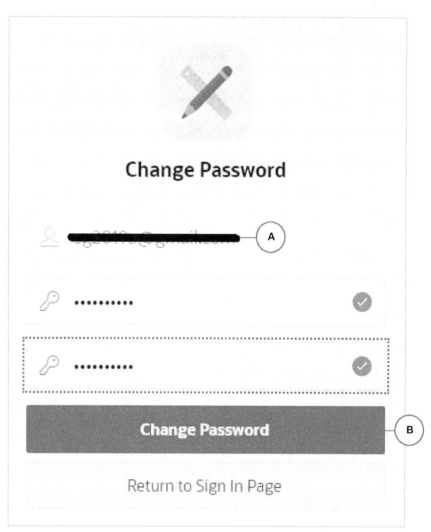

1.5 Workspace Home Page

Here you go! Your Workspace Home Page comes up resembling the following figure. It contains a top menu and four large icons to access different segments of Oracle APEX. To leave the Oracle APEX environment, click your name (appearing at top-right) and click the Sign out button.

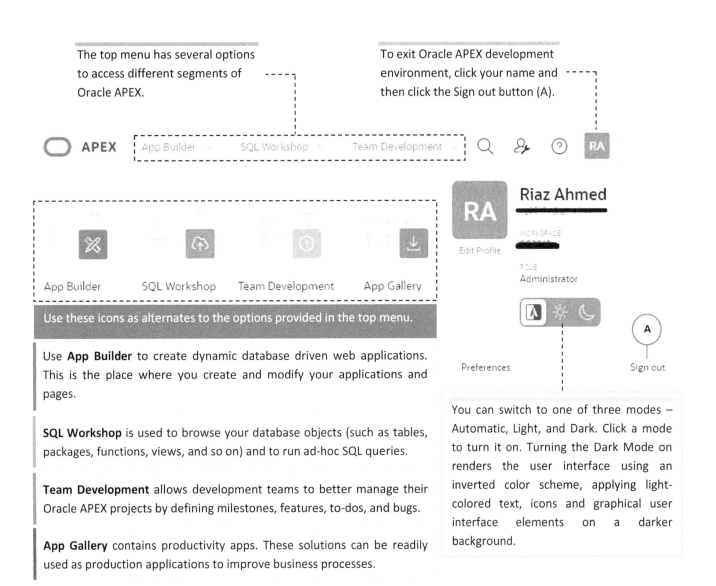

The top menu has several options to access different segments of Oracle APEX.

To exit Oracle APEX development environment, click your name and then click the Sign out button (A).

Use these icons as alternates to the options provided in the top menu.

App Builder   SQL Workshop   Team Development   App Gallery

Riaz Ahmed

Edit Profile

WORKSPACE

ROLE
Administrator

Preferences

Sign out

Use **App Builder** to create dynamic database driven web applications. This is the place where you create and modify your applications and pages.

SQL Workshop is used to browse your database objects (such as tables, packages, functions, views, and so on) and to run ad-hoc SQL queries.

Team Development allows development teams to better manage their Oracle APEX projects by defining milestones, features, to-dos, and bugs.

App Gallery contains productivity apps. These solutions can be readily used as production applications to improve business processes.

You can switch to one of three modes – Automatic, Light, and Dark. Click a mode to turn it on. Turning the Dark Mode on renders the user interface using an inverted color scheme, applying light-colored text, icons and graphical user interface elements on a darker background.

1.6 Sign In To Your Workspace

After creating a workspace you need to sign in to it to access Oracle APEX development environment using a specific URL. If you are already signed in to your workspace, sign out as instructed in the previous section and close your browser window.

Open a new browser session and type the following URL in the address bar:
https://apex.oracle.com/pls/apex/f?p=4550

Oracle APEX Sign In form will pop up on your screen, as illustrated in the following screenshot. Bookmark this page because you will have to access this page several times during this course. Input your workspace, email address, and password information you set in the previous steps in relevant boxes in the sign in form, and hit the Sign In button. You will land on your workspace home page, as illustrated in the previous screenshot. For your convenience, Oracle APEX has provided a checkbox to remember your workspace and username. If you turn this checkbox on, your workspace and username info will be shown automatically and you just need to provide your password the next time you access this page.

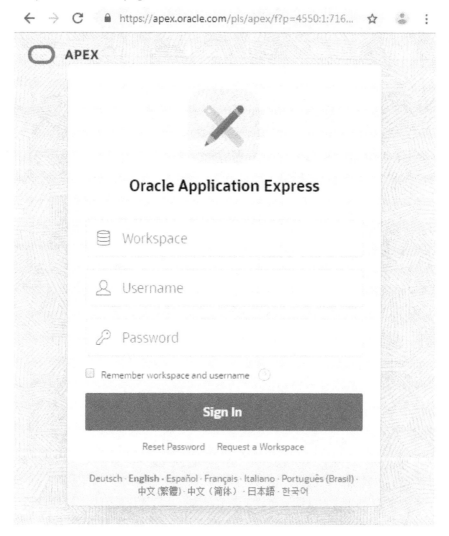

1.7 Creating Application

An application in Oracle APEX comprises one or more pages. You can create multiple applications in a single workspace. In this section you will create the barebones of your first application, which will have some auto-generated pages. You will make this application fully functional in chapter 3.

STEP 9

On the workspace home page, click the **App Builder** icon (A). On the App Builder page, click the **Create** icon (B). On the Create Application page, click the **New Application** option (C). This option will enable you to create pages on existing data. Note that you will create tables for this app in the next chapter to store data.

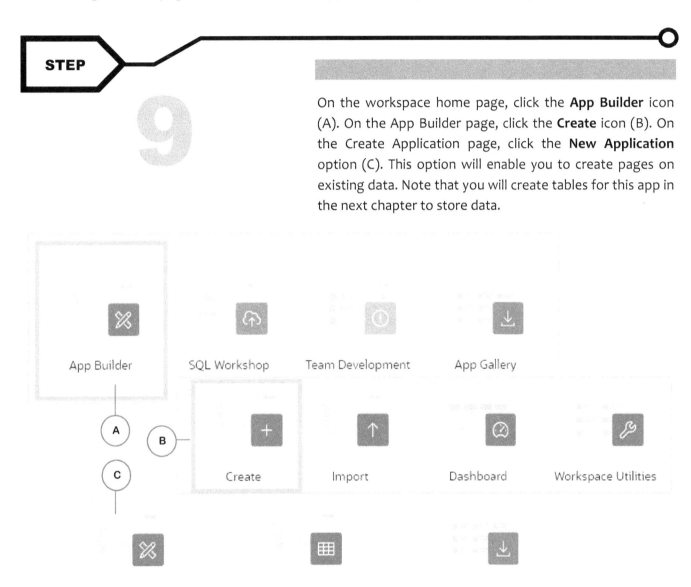

App Builder   SQL Workshop   Team Development   App Gallery

Create   Import   Dashboard   Workspace Utilities

New Application

Add pages on existing data, select application features, set your theme, and configure other options.

From a File

Upload a CSV, XLSX, XML or JSON file, or copy and paste data, then create your application.

Productivity App

Install one of many included Sample and Productivity Apps from the App Gallery.

STEP

10

Enter **Students Management System** in the Name box (A). In the Name attribute you provide a short descriptive name for an application to distinguish it from other applications in a workspace. In the Appearance section, click the icon labeled **Set Appearance** (B). On the Appearance page, select **Vita** or any other Theme Style. In the Navigation section, keep the default option **Side Menu** selected. Click the **Choose New Icon** button (C), and select a color and icon for your application from the Choose Application Icon page. After making your selection, click the **Set Application Icon** button to confirm you selections. Click **Save Changes** on the Appearance page. Finally, click the large **Create Application** button (D) to complete this process.

Create an Application

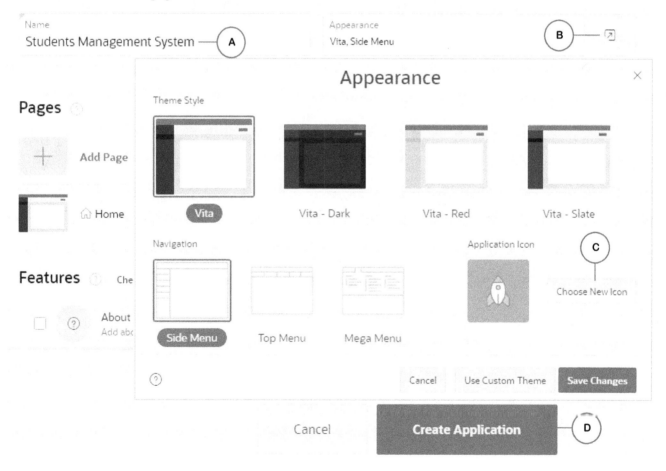

1.8 The Application Home Page

The Application home page, as illustrated in the following figure, is used to run, edit, import, export, copy, or delete an application. Select a page to edit the page properties, or click Create Page to add a page to the application.

A. Oracle APEX will create the application with three default pages – Page 1 (Home), Page 9999 (Login Page) and Page 0 (Global Page).

B. Using the Icon and Report View buttons, you can get different views of this interface. The following screen shot presents the report view.

C. You can see the ID and name of your application at the top of this page. The ID of my application is 121878.

D. To modify properties of your application (for example, application name), click the *Edit Application Properties* button.

E. Use the *Delete this Application* link in the Tasks pane to delete the current application.

F. The link *Copy this Application* creates an exact copy of the current application with a different ID.

G. You will use the *Create Page* button in subsequent chapters to create new pages in this application.

H. The *Run Application* icon runs current application in a new browser tab. Click this button to test the app.

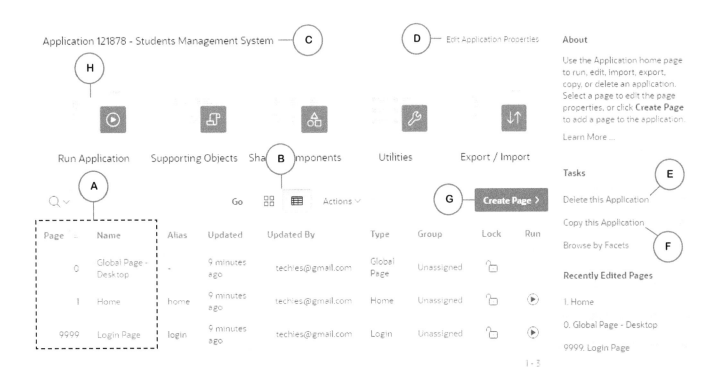

1.9 Sign In To Your Application

When you run your application, you see the application Login page in a new browser tab or window. The application sign in page is different from the workspace sign in page in that it doesn't need your workspace ID. After authenticating your credentials you are taken to the application Home page, as illustrated and briefed in the following screenshot.

The new browser window will show the Home page of your application. This page is also created by the App Builder.

This is application title. You can also display a logo along with the title via User Interface tab on the Edit Application Definition page.

The ID of the logged in user is displayed in the navigation bar. If you click the ID, you will see the Sign Out link to leave the application.

Use this icon to show/hide application menu.

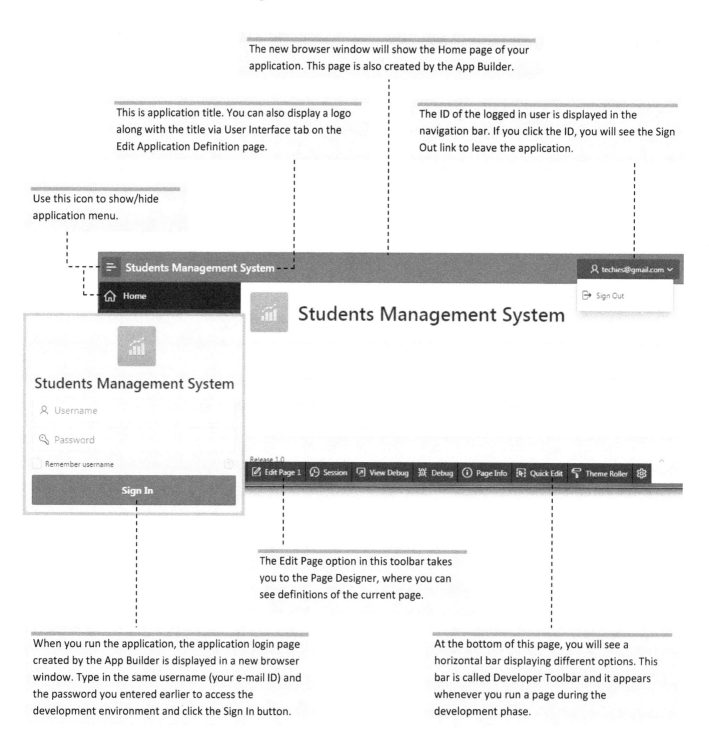

The Edit Page option in this toolbar takes you to the Page Designer, where you can see definitions of the current page.

When you run the application, the application login page created by the App Builder is displayed in a new browser window. Type in the same username (your e-mail ID) and the password you entered earlier to access the development environment and click the Sign In button.

At the bottom of this page, you will see a horizontal bar displaying different options. This bar is called Developer Toolbar and it appears whenever you run a page during the development phase.

2

Play With Oracle Database Objects Interactively

2.1 Database and Database Management System

We interact with many databases in our daily lives to get some information. For example, a phone book is a database of names and phone numbers, and an email list is a database of customer names and email addresses. A database can simply be defined as a collection of individual named objects (such as tables) to organize data.

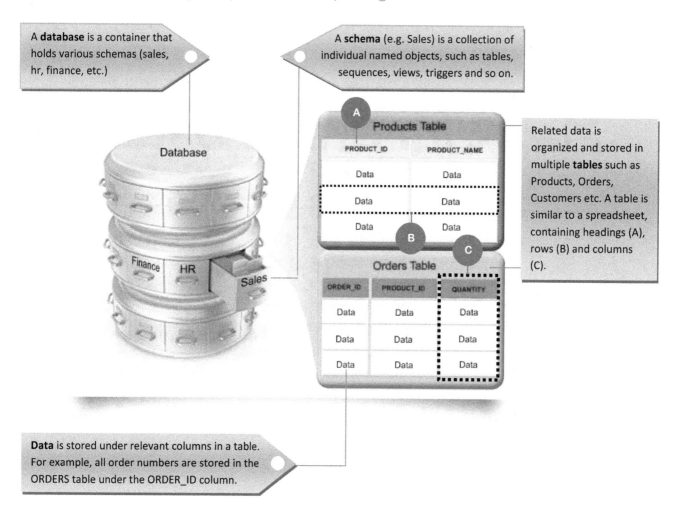

A **database** is a container that holds various schemas (sales, hr, finance, etc.)

A **schema** (e.g. Sales) is a collection of individual named objects, such as tables, sequences, views, triggers and so on.

Related data is organized and stored in multiple **tables** such as Products, Orders, Customers etc. A table is similar to a spreadsheet, containing headings (A), rows (B) and columns (C).

Data is stored under relevant columns in a table. For example, all order numbers are stored in the ORDERS table under the ORDER_ID column.

File cabinets used in an organization that carry folders and name tags are examples of paper database. From technology viewpoint, this kind of organized information handling is performed by special computer software, called database management system (DBMS).

And just as file cabinets come in many different colors and sizes, each DBMS available today has its own characteristics. A good understanding of these characteristics will help you make better use of your DBMS. In this book, you will interact with Oracle DBMS to hold your app data.

2.2 Database Tables & Relationship

A relational database organizes data in tables under individual schemas. Each table comprises columns and rows. Columns report different categories (headings) of data, and rows contain the actual vales for each column. Relationship among database tables is formed with the help of Primary, Foreign, and Composite keys. The following figure illustrates an example of a related database containing two tables.

Primary Key

A primary key is a column or a set of columns in a database table that uniquely identifies each record in that table. In order to keep data integrity, every table must have a primary key. A primary key cannot be NULL and must not allow duplicates. In the following figure, the PRODUCT_ID column in the PRODUCTS table is a primary key because it holds a unique value for each product. Besides unique identification of records, values in the primary key are used to create relationship with other database tables. Note that the PRODUCTS table has a single column primary key.

Foreign Key

You create relationship among database tables using matching columns. The figure below displays how PRODUCT_ID 1 and PRODUCT_ID 2 in the Products table relate to ORDER_ID 1000 in the Orders table. A primary key column in another table which creates a relationship between the two tables is called a foreign key. PRODUCT_ID is a foreign key in the ORDERS table. The foreign key value must exist in the table where it is a primary key. For instance, if you try to add a new order for PRODUCT_ID 4, the insert process will fail because there is no primary record for PRODUCT_ID 4 in the Products table.

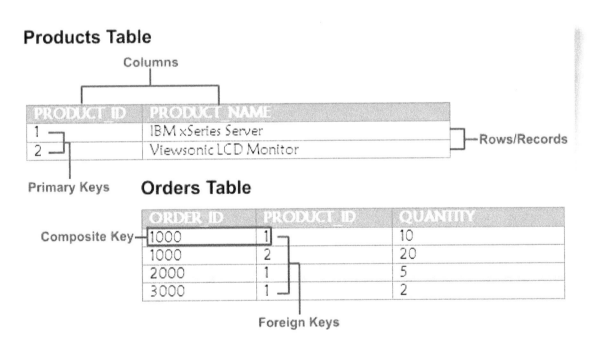

Composite Key

It is a set of columns in a table combined together to form a unique primary key. As you can see in the above figure, the first two records in the ORDERS table carry 1000 for both records, so the ORDER_ID value is not unique for these records. However, combining ORDER_ID and PRODUCT_ID columns will create a unique primary key in the Orders table, which is called a composite key. With this combination you use same ORDER_ID multiple times (for example, 1000 in the ORDERS table), but cannot add a product twice in the same order.

2.3 Data Types in Table Columns

When you create a table, you provide column names (such as, STUDENT_ID, STUDENT_NAME and so on) and their data types that act as the table's structure. Each column in a table has an associated data type, which specifies what type of data the column can contain. In this book, you will use the following basic data types.

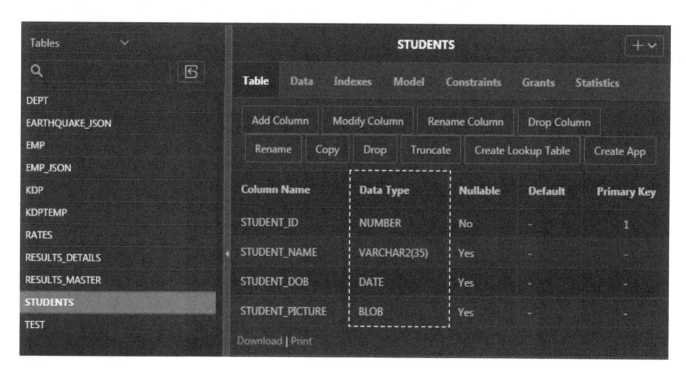

If the column were to contain a number (quantity of items in an order), the data type would be a numeric data type. For text information, the appropriate data type would be VARCHAR2 or CHAR. And, to store date information, DATE or TIMESTAMP types should be used.

The BLOB type is used to store digitized information, such as images. You select relevant data types to also restrict the type of data that can be stored in a column (for instance, to prevent recording of alphabetical or special characters into a monetary column).

2.4 Object Browser

In Oracle APEX, the Object Browser is a tool under SQL Workshop menu which is used to review and maintain database objects (such as, tables, functions, triggers and so on).

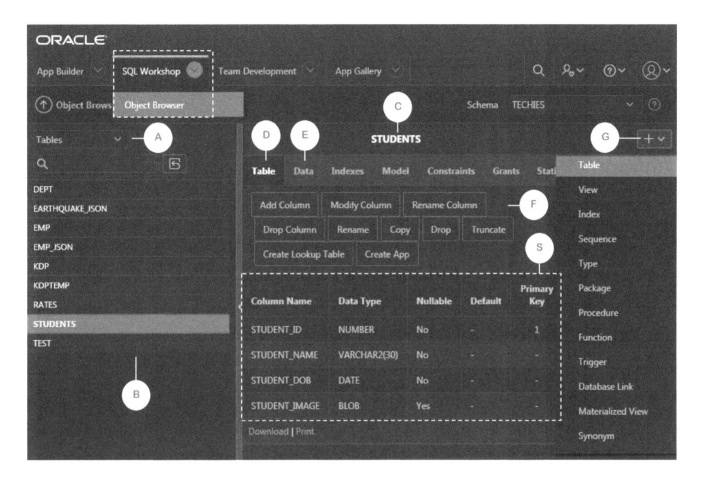

A. This is a select list from where you choose a database object category from a dozen objects. By default, you see the Tables option.

B. The objects of the selected category are displayed in this pane. For example, if you select Tables from the select list, all tables in the current schema will appear in this pane.

C. You see the selected object's details here. For example, if you select the Students table in the left pane, the details of this table are shown in this area.

D. The Table tab displays the selected table's structure (S).

E. Clicking the Data tab displays data in the selected table.

F. Using these buttons you manipulate structure of the selected table. In addition to manipulating column structures, you can also rename and drop the table using the Rename and Drop buttons.

G. The Create menu lets you create new database objects that you will do next.

2.5 Creating Database Tables

Developers create database tables by executing SQL's CREATE TABLE statement in SQL Commands interface. However, Oracle APEX also cares for non-developers and allows them to create, modify, and drop all database objects interactively. Let's create three tables for our app using SQL Workshop's Object Browser interface. The first table will hold students' profiles, while the remaining two tables will store their results information. The last step in this exercise will invoke a wizard (discussed next) that will walk you through to interactively create your first database table without writing any SQL statement.

1. Click the **SQL Workshop** menu.

2. Select the **Object Browser** option from the menu, which is used to review and maintain database objects (such as, tables, sequences, views, functions, triggers, and so on).

3. In the Object Browser page, select the **Tables** option from the select list. This action will show a list of existing tables in the left pane, if there are any.

4. Click the **Create** menu, and select **Table** from the menu list to create a new table. This will invoke a wizard named Create Table, discussed next.

2.5.1 Students Table

The Create Table wizard comprises five steps. The first step is named Columns (as illustrated in the following figure) in which you specify the name of your new table and its basic structure, which includes column names, their types, and respective sizes.

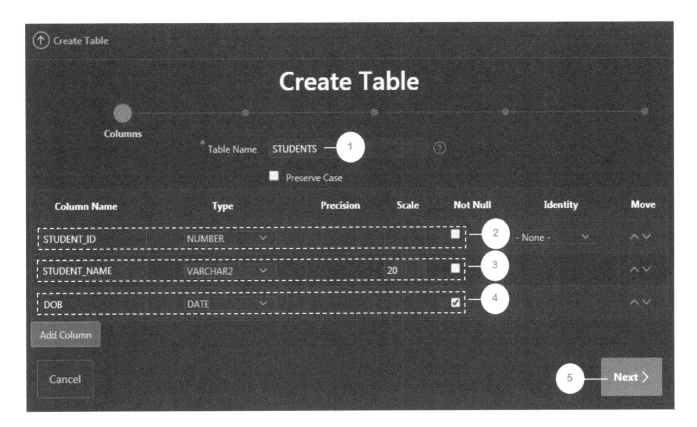

1. Enter **STUDENTS** for Table Name.

2. Enter **STUDENT_ID** in the first Column Name and select **NUMBER** from the Type select list. Each student will have a unique auto-generated numeric ID and this column will store that ID.

3. Enter **STUDENT_NAME** in the second Column Name. Select **VARCHAR2** as its Type and enter **20** in the Scale box which means each student's name must be less than or equal to twenty characters. The VARCHAR2 type column stores variable-length character strings, such as name, address, and so on.

4. In the third row, enter **DOB** for Column Name, and select **DATE** as its Type. This column will store students' birth dates. Click the **Not Null** checkbox representing the DOB column to place a check mark, which makes the column mandatory at table level. Note that a validation check will be created for this and other columns in your app as well. For primary key columns (see the next section) the Not Null constraint is turned on automatically.

5. Click the **Next** button to move on to the second wizard screen.

2.5.1.1 Specify Primary Key

The next wizard screen titled Primary Key collects information about the primary key of this table, which is a column in your table to uniquely identify each record and to prevent duplicates. The primary keys in the Students table will be populated automatically with the help of a database object named Sequence.

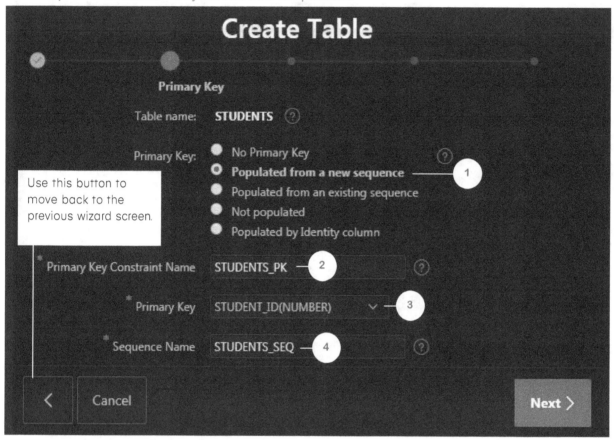

1. From the Primary Key options, select **Populated from a new sequence**. As you click this option, three additional fields pop up on your screen.

2. Enter or accept **STUDENT_PK** for the *Primary Key Constraint Name*. You can specify any other name if you wish to. This is the name of your primary key constraint to uniquely identify each row/record in the Students table.

3. For Primary Key, select **STUDENT_ID** from the adjacent list. This is the column that will act as the primary key to uniquely identify each record in the table.

4. Accept the name of the default Sequence Name or enter any other name. A Sequence is a database object which generates unique integer values automatically. Here, it will generate unique primary keys for each student's record, and these values will be stored in the STUDENT_ID column. Press the **Next** button thrice skipping Foreign Key and Constraints wizard screens. On the final Confirm screen, click the **Create Table** button.

2.5.1.2 Examine Sequence and Constraint

After creating the table, you are landed back to the Object Browser page displaying the Students table and its structure. Let's examine a couple of objects that the wizard generated behind the scenes to handle data in this table.

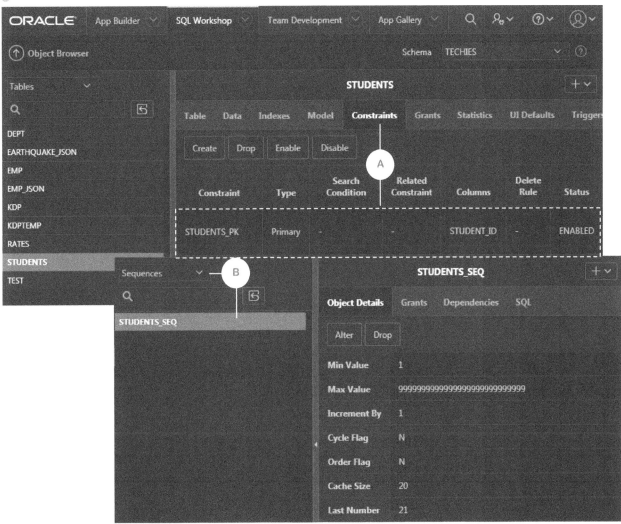

A. Click the **Constraints** tab. You will see the STUDENTS_PK constraint you defined on the previous page to mark the STUDENT_ID column as the primary key for the table.

B. Next, from the dropdown list, choose **Sequences**. The STUDENTS_SEQ sequence, also defined on the previous page, will appear with its details in the right pane. It has 1 as the minimum value, meaning that the first record's ID in the STUDENTS table will have this value.

2.5.1.3 Manipulate Table Structure

You can modify the structure of a table after its creation. Let's use the bunch of buttons appearing in the right pane just above the table structure to test their respective functionalities. Refer to the figure presented in section 2.4 – Object Browser.

Add Column: Click the **Add Column** button to add a new column to the table. This column is of BLOB type to store students' pictures.

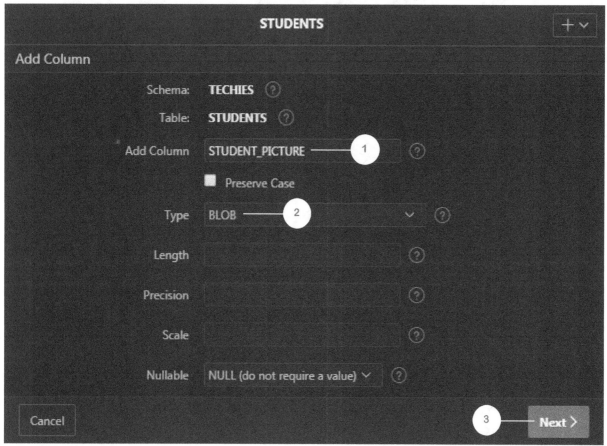

1. On the Add Column screen, enter **STUDENT_PICTURE** for the *Add Column* field.

2. Set the *Type* of this new column to **BLOB** (Binary Large OBjects), an Oracle data type that can hold up to 4 GB of data. BLOBs are handy for storing digitized information, such as images, audio, and video. You can also store your document files like PDF, MS Word, MS Excel, MS PowerPoint and CSV to name a few.

3. Click **Next** and then **Finish**. The new column will be appended to the table structure.

Modify Column: You can modify the data type and size of an existing column. Click the **Modify Column** button to alter the size of the STUDENT_NAME column.

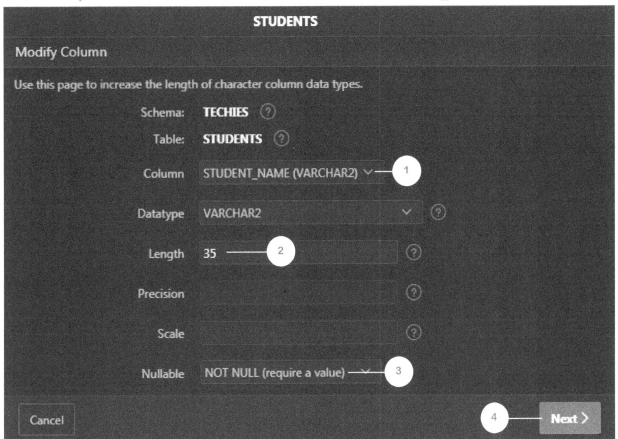

1. On the Modify Column screen, select the **STUDENT_NAME** column from the *Column* list.

2. Change its existing *Length* value from 20 to **35**. This will increase the length of the column. Now the column will accept names up to 35 characters.

3. From the Nullable list, select **NOT NULL (require a value)** to ensure that this column is not left blank. This is an alternate method for setting the Not Null constraint for a column, if you forgot to set it initially. Recall that you set this constraint for the DOB column earlier in this chapter while creating the STUDENTS table.

4. Click **Next** and then **Finish**. The length of this column will now be shown as VARCHAR2(35) on the Object Browser page.

Rename Column: You can also change the name of an existing column. Click the **Rename Column** button to rename the DOB (Date of Birth) column.

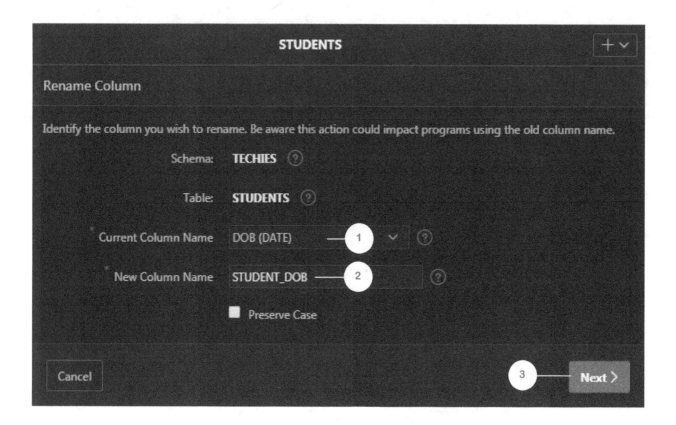

1. On the Rename Column screen, select the **DOB** column from the *Current Column Name* list.

2. In the *New Column Name* field, enter **STUDENT_DOB** to set it as the new name for the column.

3. Click **Next** and then **Finish**. The column will be renamed and the new name will be displayed on the Object Browser page.

Drop Column: Using the Drop Column button you can delete an existing column. To test the functionality of this button, you have to add a new column. Set any name and type for the new column – I named mine as TEST. After adding this column, click the **Drop Column** button to see the following screen.

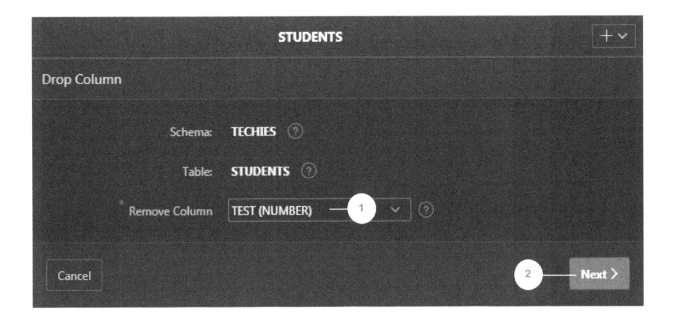

1. On the Drop Column screen, select the new column from the *Remove Column* list.

2. Click **Next** and then **Finish**. The column will be removed from the table structure on the Object Browser page.

2.5.1.4 Manipulating Data Interactively

Developers usually execute SQL's DML (Data Manipulation Language) statements to view, insert, update, and delete records in a table. But Oracle APEX allows you to perform all these operations interactively without any code.

Add Data: Let's see how to insert a record in the STUDENTS table without writing SQL's INSERT statement.

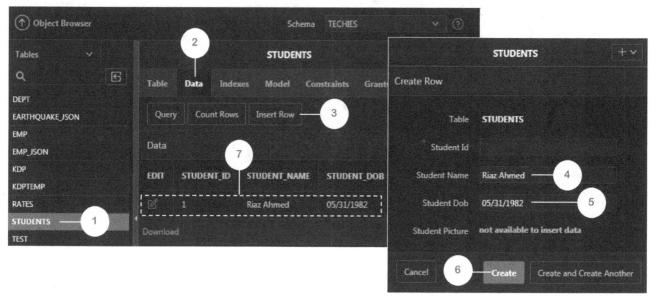

1. On the Object Browser page, click the **STUDENTS** table in the left pane.

2. In the right pane, click the **Data** tab. When you click the Data tab, you see data in the selected table. Right now there is not data in the table so nothing appears on the screen.

3. Click the **Insert Row** button. This will bring up the Create Row page.

4. Leaving the Student Id field blank, type your name in the Student Name field.

5. In the Student Dob field, enter your date of birth in mm/dd/yyyy format.

6. Click the **Create** button to create this record in the STUDENTS table. The other button labeled *Create and Create Another* saves the current record and makes the input form blank to accept another record. Note that the *Student Picture* field is freeze here because you cannot add an image via this form – you will do that in a subsequent chapter.

7. When you get back to the Object Browser screen, a record appears with 1 in the STUDENT_ID column. This is the ID which is generated and put in the table automatically by the STUDENT_SEQ sequence object.

Modify and Delete Data: You can also update or delete a record interactively without using SQL's UPDATE or DELETE statements. Both these operations are performed through one screen, as illustrated in the following figure.

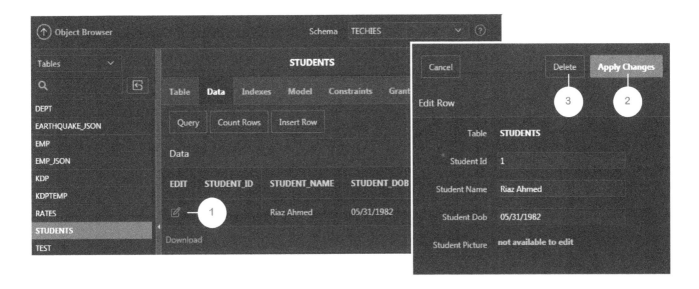

1. On the Data tab, click the **Edit** icon.

2. Modify data in the Edit Row screen. For example, change student's name or date of birth. After the modification, click the **Apply Changes** button to save your changes.

3. To delete a record from the table, use the same Edit icon to view the record in the Edit Row screen. Then, click the Delete button. Clicking the **Delete** button now will remove the solitary record in the table. Note that you will populate the STUDENTS table with data through your application later in this book.

2.5.2 Results Master and Details Tables

In this exercise you will learn how to create relational tables. You will create two tables named RESULTS_MASTER and RESULTS_DETAILS to store students' results information. The master table will store header information, such as STUDENT_ID and academic session, while the details table will store marks information by subject, obtained by each student. The two tables will be joined together via Primary Key and Foreign Key relationship. In addition, the RESULTS_MASTER table will also be joined with the STUDENTS table to create a relationship between these tables as well.

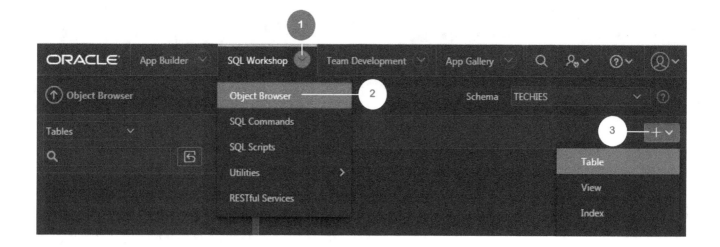

1. Click the **SQL Workshop** menu.

2. Select the **Object Browser** option from the menu.

3. Click the **Create** menu, and select **Table** from the menu list to create a new table. Once again, the Create Table wizard will be launched.

Provide name for the master table and enter column information as follows.

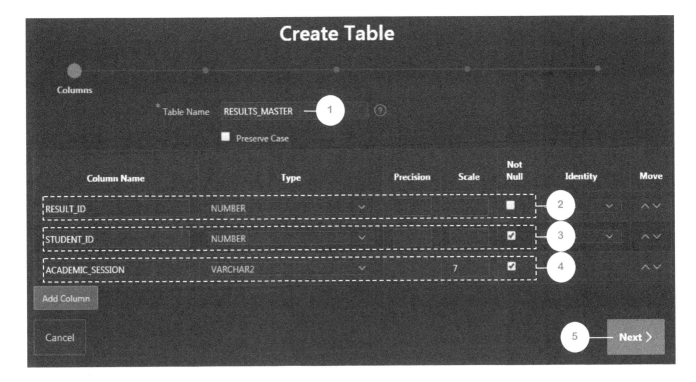

1. Enter **RESULTS_MASTER** for Table Name.

2. Enter **RESULT_ID** in the first Column Name and select **NUMBER** from the Type select list. Each student's result recorded in this table will have a unique auto-generated numeric ID.

3. Enter **STUDENT_ID** in the second Column Name. Select **NUMBER** as its Type. Turn on the **Not Null** constraint. The STUDENTS table will be linked to the RESULTS_MASTER table via this column. The relationship between the two tables will be created in a moment.

4. In the third row, enter **ACADEMIC_SESSION** for Column Name, and select **VARCHAR2** as its Type. Enter **7** in the Scale field and turn on the **Not Null** constraint. This column will store students' results by academic session in 9999-99 format.

5. Click the **Next** button to proceed.

Provide Primary Key information. The primary keys for this table will also be generated from a database sequence named RESULTS_MASTER_SEQ to populate the RESULT_ID column, which is the primary key for this table.

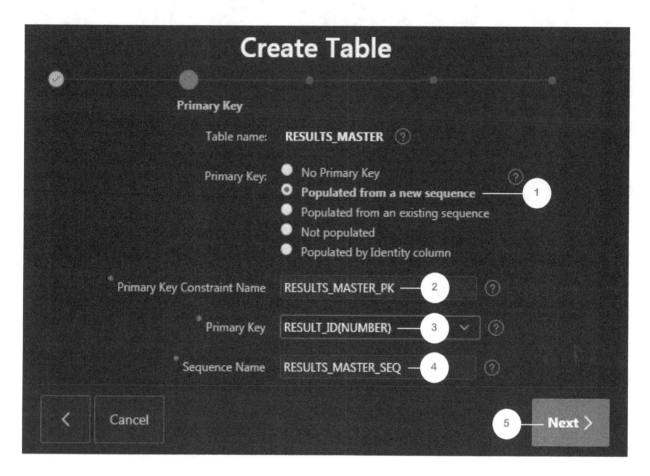

1. Once again, select **Populated from a new sequence** option from the *Primary Key* options.

2. Accept **RESULTS_MASTER_PK** for the *Primary Key Constraint Name*.

3. For the Primary Key, select the **RESULT_ID** column.

4. Accept the default Sequence Name (**RESULTS_MASTER_SEQ**) or enter any other name. The RESULT_ID primary key column in this table will receive auto-generated keys from this sequence object.

5. Press the **Next** button.

The next wizard screen collects information about Foreign Key. A foreign key establishes a relationship between a column or columns in one table and a primary or unique key in another table. Here, you are establishing a relationship between the STUDENTS and RESULTS_MASTER tables.

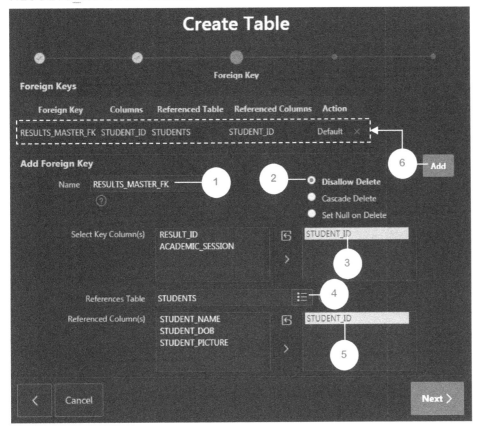

After creating this table, click the Constraints tab in the Object Browser page. The tab will show two constraints for this table. The RESULTS_MASTER_PK is the Primary Key constraint which is created to uniquely identify each record. The RESULTS_MASTER_FK is the foreign key constraint that will prevent accidental deletion of students' records if they are referenced in this table.

1. Accept the default name (**RESULTS_MASTER_FK**) for the foreign key constraint name.

2. The default **Disallow Delete** option will block deletion of rows from the STUDENTS table when they are utilized in the RESULTS_MASTER table.

3. From the left pane in the *Select Key Column(s)* section, move the **STUDENT_ID** column to the right pane using the single right-arrow icon (>). This action specifies that the STUDENT_ID column in this table is a foreign key and has a reference in some other table.

4. Click the icon next to the *References Table*, and pick the **STUDENTS** table. All columns from this table will appear in the *Referenced Column(s)* left pane.

5. In the Referenced Column(s) section, move the **STUDENT_ID** column to the right pane. Here you are telling APEX that this is the column in the STUDENTS table that will be referenced by the STUDENT_ID column in the RESULTS_MASTER table. Now the two tables have a relationship based on the STUDENT_ID column.

6. Click the **Add** button. The details of the FK constraint will appear on the page. Press the **Next** button twice, and then click the **Create Table** button on the *Confirm* screen to complete the process.

Here are the steps to create the RESULT_DETAILS table. This table will store each student's marks by subject.

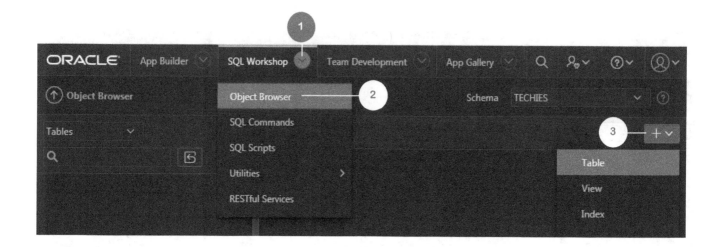

1. Click the **SQL Workshop** menu.

2. Select the **Object Browser** option from the menu.

3. Click the **Create** menu, and select **Table** from the menu list to create a new table. Once again, the Create Table wizard will be launched.

Provide name for the details table and enter column information as follows.

1. Enter **RESULTS_DETAILS** for Table Name.

2. Enter **LINE_NO** in the first Column Name and select **Number** from the Type list. This is the primary key for the table.

3. Enter **RESULT_ID** in the second Column Name and select **NUMBER** from the Type select list. This column will act as a foreign key to establish relationship with the RESULTS_MASTER table.

4. Enter **SUBJECT** in the third Column Name. Select **VARCHAR2** as its Type. For this tutorial, you will store Maths, Physics, and Language subjects in this column.

5. In the next row, enter **MARKS** for Column Name, and select **NUMBER** as its Type. Enter **6** in the Precision text box and **2** in the Scale field. This column will store the obtained marks in the selected subject in 999.99 format – for example, 82.50. Where, 82 is precision and 50, after the decimal place, is scale.

6. Click the **Next** button to proceed.

Provide Primary Key information. The primary keys for this table will also be generated from a database sequence named RESULTS_DETAIL_SEQ to populate the LINE_NO primary key column.

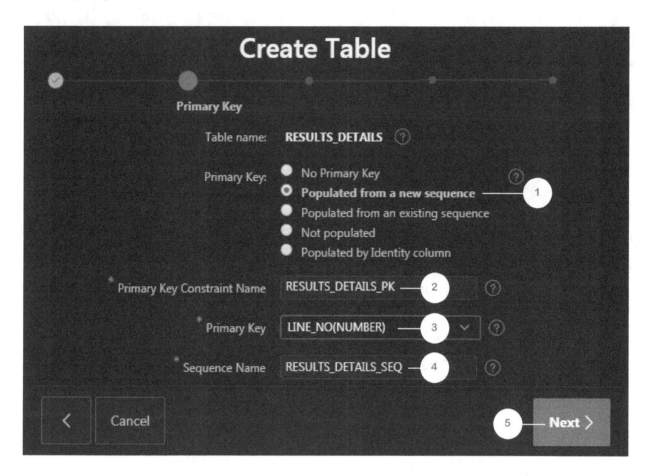

1. Again, select **Populated from a new sequence** option from the *Primary Key* options.

2. Accept **RESULTS_DETAILS_PK** for the *Primary Key Constraint Name*.

3. Select the **LINE_NO** column from the Primary Key list.

4. Accept the default Sequence Name (**RESULTS_DETAILS_SEQ**) or enter any other name. The LINE_NO primary key column in this table will receive auto-generated keys from this sequence object.

5. Press the **Next** button.

Enter Foreign Key information as follows to establish a relationship between the RESULTS_MASTER and RESULTS_DETAILS tables.

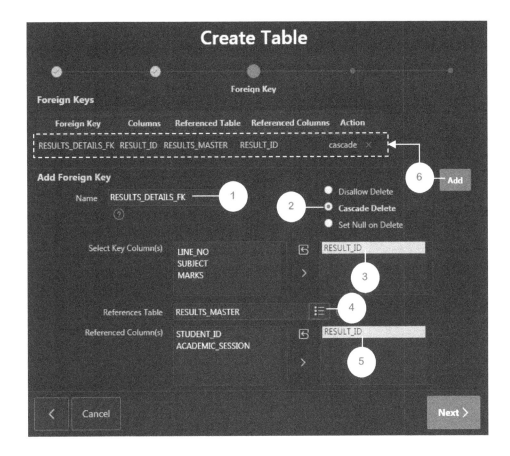

After creating this table, click the Constraints tab in the Object Browser page and view the two constraints you just created.

1. Accept the default name (**RESULTS_DETAILS_FK**) for the foreign key constraint name.

2. For this table select the **Cascade Delete** option, which deletes the dependant rows from this table when the corresponding row is deleted from the RESULTS_MASTER table.

3. From the left pane in the *Select Key Column(s)* section, move the **RESULT_ID** column to the right pane using the single right-arrow icon (>). This action specifies that the RESULT_ID column in this table is a foreign key and has a reference in the master table.

4. Select the **RESULTS_MASTER** table for the *References Table*. All columns from this table will appear in the *Referenced Column(s)* left pane.

5. Move the **RESULT_ID** column to the right pane.

6. Click the **Add** button. The details of the FK constraint will appear on the page. Press the **Next** button twice, and then click the **Create Table** button on the *Confirm* screen to complete the process.

2.5.3 Relationship Diagram

The relationship among the three tables you created in this exercise for your application is presented in the following diagram.

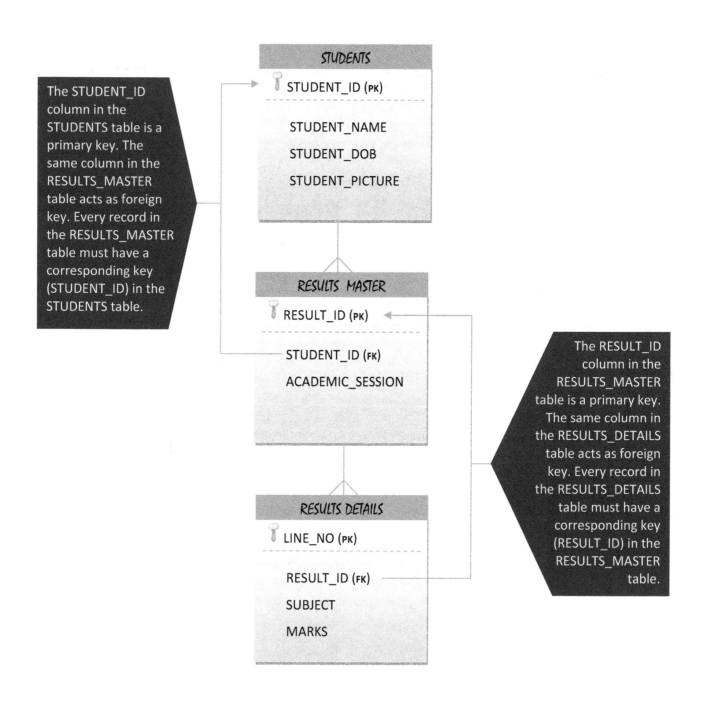

The STUDENT_ID column in the STUDENTS table is a primary key. The same column in the RESULTS_MASTER table acts as foreign key. Every record in the RESULTS_MASTER table must have a corresponding key (STUDENT_ID) in the STUDENTS table.

STUDENTS
- STUDENT_ID (PK)
- STUDENT_NAME
- STUDENT_DOB
- STUDENT_PICTURE

RESULTS MASTER
- RESULT_ID (PK)
- STUDENT_ID (FK)
- ACADEMIC_SESSION

The RESULT_ID column in the RESULTS_MASTER table is a primary key. The same column in the RESULTS_DETAILS table acts as foreign key. Every record in the RESULTS_DETAILS table must have a corresponding key (RESULT_ID) in the RESULTS_MASTER table.

RESULTS DETAILS
- LINE_NO (PK)
- RESULT_ID (FK)
- SUBJECT
- MARKS

2.5.4 Testing Relationship

Let's do some testing on the three tables to evaluate the relationships we created in the previous exercises.

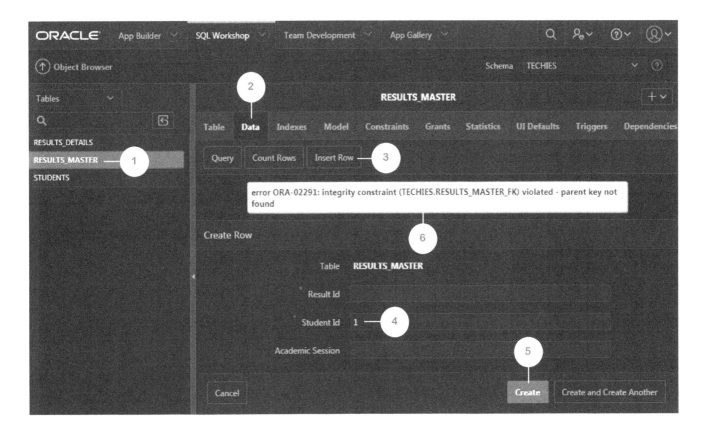

NOTE: Before executing the following instructions, make sure that the STUDENTS table is empty. If it contains some records, delete them using the instructions provided in section 2.5.1.4 - Modify and Delete Data - step 3.

1. Click the **RESULTS_MASTER** table in the left pane.

2. Click the **Data** tab.

3. Click the **Insert Row** button to add a record to this table.

4. Enter **1** in the Student Id field. Enter **abc** in the Academic Session field.

5. Click the **Create** button to save this record.

6. You'll see an error mentioning that the RESULTS_MASTER_FK foreign constraint is violated. The error is encountered because the number (1) you entered for the Student ID doesn't exist in the STUDENTS table – the table is blank at the moment.

Now, click the **STUDENTS** table in the left pane and insert a row – see section 2.5.1.4. After creating the record in the STUDENTS table, take a note of the STUDENT_ID value and repeat step 1 through 5 in this exercise. Enter the student id (you just noted) in the Student Id field (4). Type some text in the Academic Session field and click the Create button. The record should now be created without any error because now we referenced an existing student ID.

Both STUDENTS and RESULTS_MASTER tables in my scenario have one record each and both have 1 in their respective STUDENT_ID columns, that is, the solitary STUDENT_ID in the STUDENTS table has a reference in the RESULTS_MASTER table. Execute the following steps and try to delete this record.

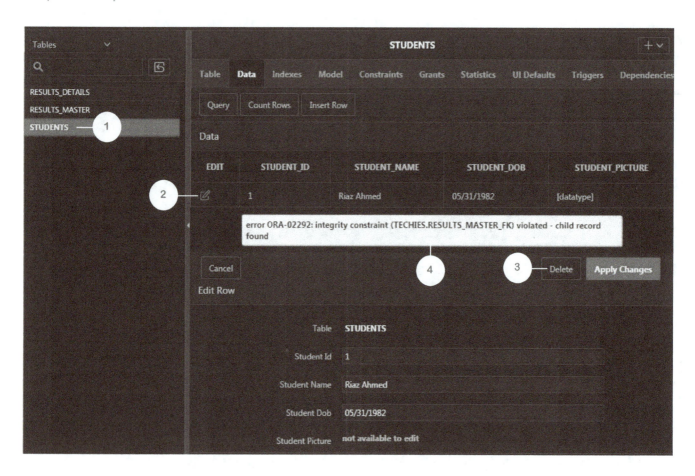

1. Select the **STUDENTS** table from the left pane.

2. On the Data tab, click the **Edit** icon.

3. On the Edit Row screen, click the **Delete** button to remove this record from the table.

4. Once again, you'll see an error message telling a different story. This time, the error occurred because it found a child record in the RESULTS_MASTER table. The parent child relationship between the two tables prevented the deletion process. The main objective behind implementing integrity constraint relationships among database tables is to prevent deletion of records from a parent table when it has corresponding records in child table(s).

Click the **RESULTS_MASTER** table in the left pane, and click the **Edit** icon on the Data tab, and delete the record in this table. Now that the reference has vanished, you can delete record from the STUDENTS table without encountering any error.

You can perform this exercise to test the relationship between RESULTS_MASTER and RESULTS_DETAILS tables. First, create a record in the master table and then, using the value in the RESULT_ID primary key column, create a corresponding child record in the RESULTS_DETAILS table. When you try to delete the master record from the RESULTS_MASTER table, you will encounter the same *child record found* error (4).

3

Create Fully Functional Application Pages Without Coding

3.1 Application Pages

A page is the basic unit of APEX applications that contains user interface elements, such as regions, items, navigation menu, lists, buttons, and more. Each page is identified by its name or a unique number. In this book you will create your application pages with the help of built-in wizards. Based on your selections, page creation wizards automatically adds components such as form, report, chart, maps and so on to a page with their layouts and business logic.

In this chapter, as well as in subsequent chapter, you will create some application pages to manage students' module. First, you will create a couple of pages comprising a report and a simple input form to manage students' profiles. These pages will be created via page creation wizard and will store data in the STUDENTS table, created in the previous chapter. The pages will allow you to:

- View and search students
- Add record of a new student to the database table (STUDENTS)
- Modify students profile
- Remove a student from the database

The first page (top in the following figure) is an interactive report, which displays a list of all students from the STUDENTS table using an auto-generated SQL SELECT query. The second one, illustrated at the bottom, is an input form which is used to receive details of new students, and modify or delete record of an existing student. The pencil icon in the first report column is a link. When you click this link, the form page appears with complete profile of the selected student.

Students Management System

Q ∨   Go   Actions ∨   **Create**

	Student Id	Student Name	Date of Birth	Student Picture
✎	121	Sarim Muavia	5/17/2011	
✎	101	Riaz Ahmed	2/20/1984	

Link to access the Students Form page

1 - 2

Students Form ⊗

Student Name
Sarim Muavia

Student Dob
5/17/2011   ▦

Student Picture
Choose file   🗁

Cancel   Delete   **Apply Changes**

Students Interactive Report Page displays a list of students from the STUDENTS table

Student's Form Page is used to add, modify and delete students' records

3.2 Create Pages to Manage Students Info

The App Builder wizard created the Home and Login pages for our application in chapter 1 Section 1.8. The rest of the pages in this application will be created interactively with the help of APEX's built-in wizards that ask you simple questions to create the page you wish to add to your application.

If you are not already logged in, log back in to Oracle APEX environment – see Chapter 1 - Section 1.6. Once you are in the APEX environment, execute the following steps to create the two pages to manage students' profiles.

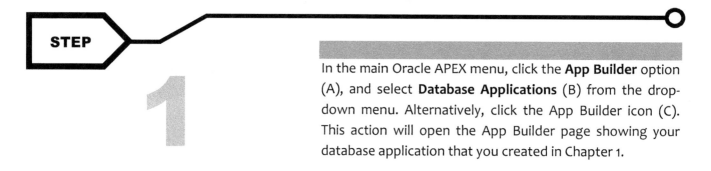

STEP

1

In the main Oracle APEX menu, click the **App Builder** option (A), and select **Database Applications** (B) from the drop-down menu. Alternatively, click the App Builder icon (C). This action will open the App Builder page showing your database application that you created in Chapter 1.

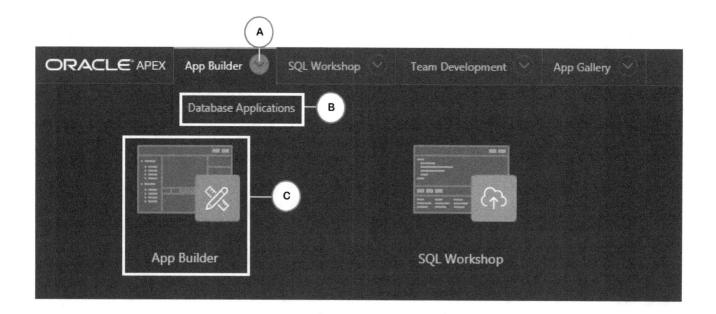

STEP

2

In the main App Builder interface, click the Students Management System's **Edit** icon (A). The application page (the lower screenshot in the following illustration) will appear on your screen. On this page, click the **Create Page** button (B). This button is used whenever you intend to create a new page in an application. The action will start the create page wizard – discussed next.

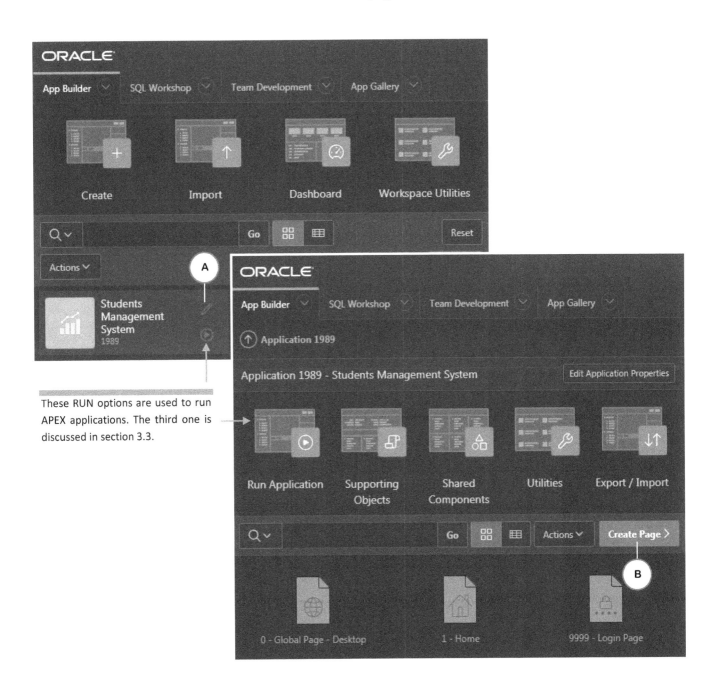

These RUN options are used to run APEX applications. The third one is discussed in section 3.3.

STEP

3

This is the first screen of the *Create a Page* wizard which displays a couple of page type categories, and multiple page options under each category.

Component pages provide page-level functionality and can be added multiple times within a given application. Examples include reports, forms, plug-ins, charts, calendar and so on.

Feature pages provide application-level functionality and are typically added once per application. Examples include About Page, Access Control, Activity Reporting, Feedback, and Login Page.

For this exercise, select the **Component** type (A), and then click the **Form** option (B).

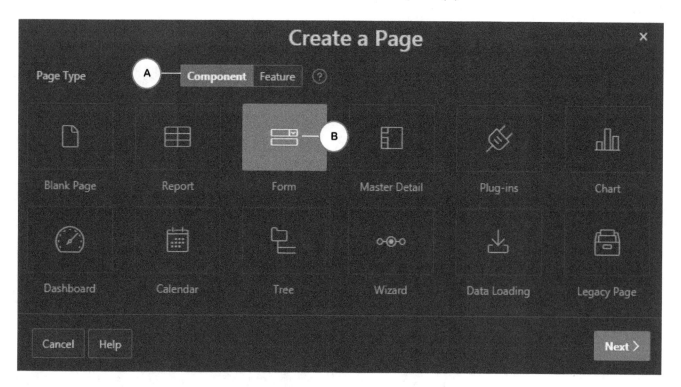

STEP

4

On the next wizard screen, click the **Report with Form** option. This screen presents sub-categories of the selected Form option. For the selected option (Report with Form), the wizard will create two pages – an interactive report and a form. The report page will display a list of students, while the form page will be used to add, update, and delete students' information, as illustrated in section 3.1.

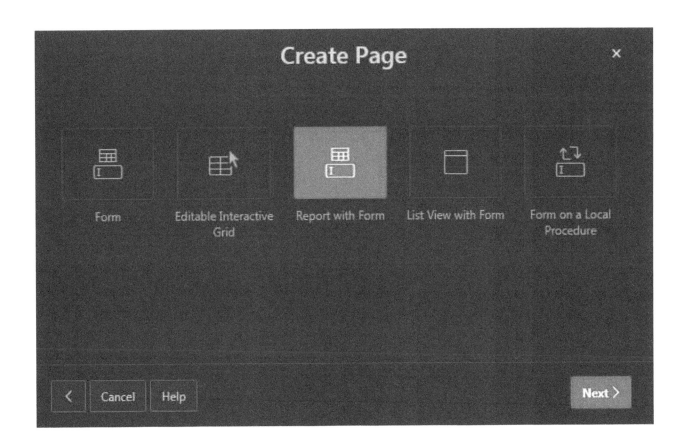

STEP

5

On the *Page Attributes* wizard screen, select options and enter values as depicted in the following screenshot and click Next.

For Report Type, we opted to create an Interactive Report (IR), which will be created using an auto-generated SQL SELECT statement. IR allows you to alter the layout of report data by selecting specific columns, applying filters, highlighting, and sorting. You can also define breaks, aggregations, different types of charts, and custom computations.

In Application Express each page is identified with a unique number. The main page of this module (which will carry an interactive report) will be recognized by number 2, whereas the form page will have number 3. Just like numbers, a page is provided with a unique name for visual recognition. You can recognize a page by its name in the App Builder interface.

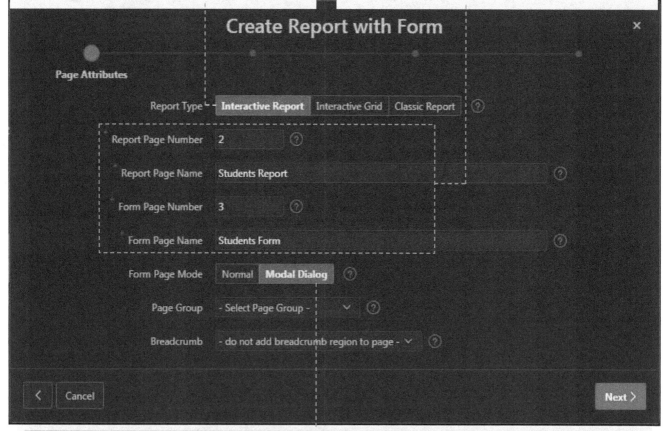

The Form Page Mode property specifies how you want to see a page. It has two options: *Normal* and *Modal Dialog*. New pages created in Oracle APEX default to *Normal*. When you call a normal page, it simply replaces existing page being displayed in your browser. A Modal Dialog page appears on top of its calling page and doesn't allow users to do anything else unless it is closed. A modal page can be displayed only on top of another page. In the current scenario, the Students Form page will appear on top of the Students Report page.

STEP

6

The next wizard screen (Navigation Menu) asks whether you want to create a navigation menu entry for this module. Select **Create a new navigation menu entry** option (A) for *Navigation Preference*. For *New Navigation menu Entry*, type **Manage Students Profiles** (B) – this is the name of the new menu entry. Do not select anything for the *Parent Navigation Menu Entry*, because this entry itself is a parent entry. Click **Next** to proceed.

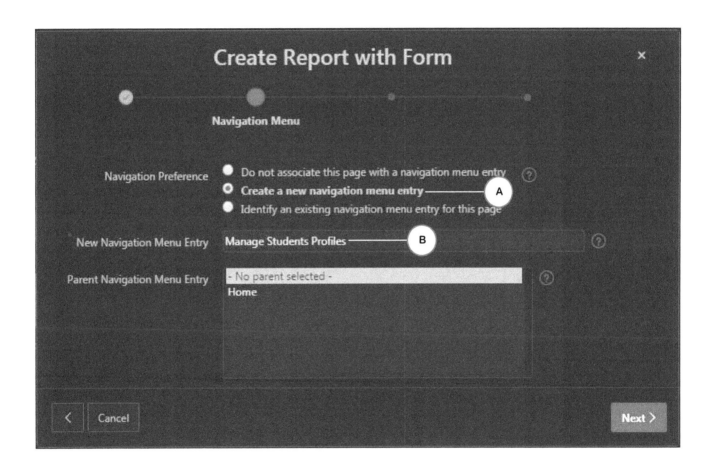

STEP

7

On the *Data Source* wizard step, you specify the backend table that will be used by this module to view, add, update, and delete data. For *Data Source*, select **Local Database** (A), because we will use the STUDENTS table from the local database. Keep the **Table** (B) *Source Type* selected. As an absolute beginner you are using this option, once you get to the next level, you can use the *SQL Query* option. The *Table/View Owner* will be displaying your current schema – TECHIES is my schema. Click the icon (C) representing *Table/View Name*, and select the **STUDENTS** table from the popup list. This is the table that will be used by this module. All the columns from this table will appear in the right pane in the *Select Columns to be shown in the report* section. If not, move all columns from the left pane to the right pane using the double arrow icon (D). Click **Next**.

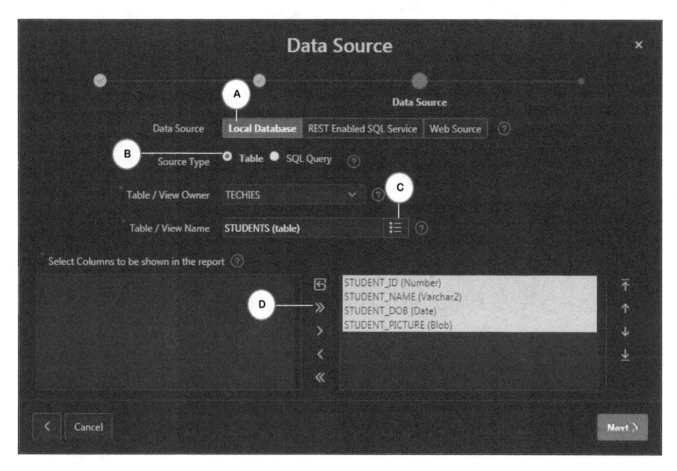

STEP

8

On the final *Form Page* screen, all table columns will appear in the right pane, which means that all these columns will appear on the data entry form. For *Primary Key Type*, select the second option – **Select Primary Key Column(s)** (A). For *Primary Key Column*, select the **STUDENT_ID** column (B). This column will be used as a primary key to handle data in the STUDENTS table. Based on this information, the wizard will create all necessary objects in the database to auto-generate ids for new students. The same key column will be used to handle update and delete operations as well. Click the **Create** button to complete the page creation process.

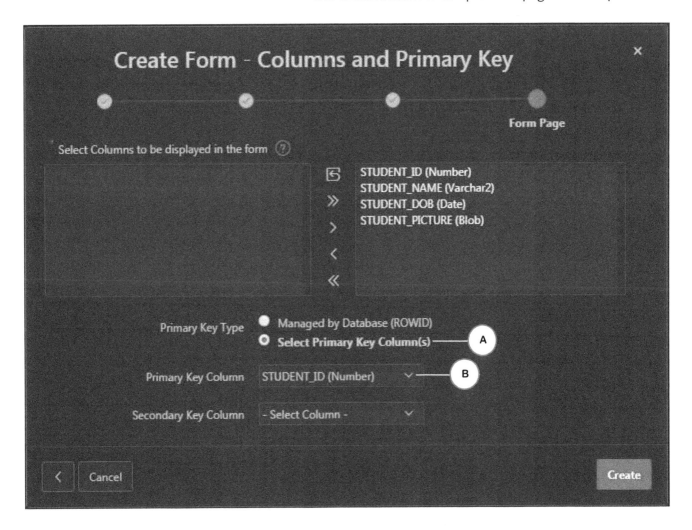

3.3 Running Application Pages

After creating the page in the previous step, you will see Page Designer interface, which displays structure of your application page. It is the main development interface where programmers manipulate page components. They use this interface to view, create, and edit page components and application logic. At his stage, it will be displaying the Students Report page (Page 2).

The Page Designer interface comprises a toolbar (A), and three panes – Tree pane, Central pane, and Property Editor. You'll learn more about this interface in detail in upcoming sections. For now, just click the **Save and Run Page** button (B). The application login screen (as illustrated on the next page) will be displayed in a new browser tab.

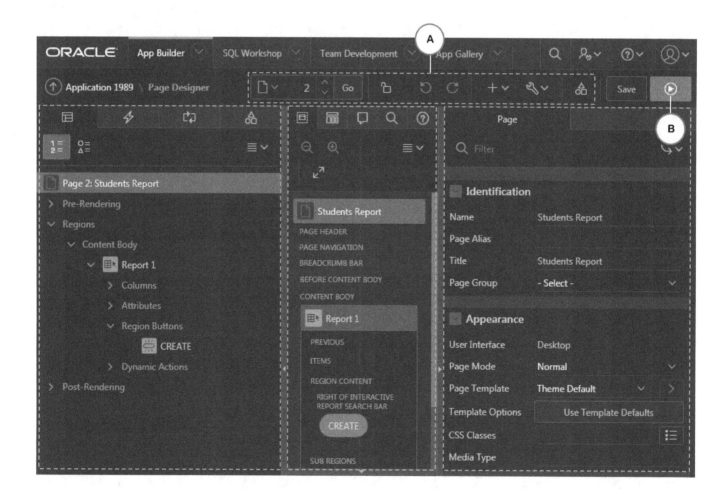

Click the Page Designer tab to access the development environment for modifications

The application runtime environment that is displayed in a new browser tab

The application URL contains your app ID (A), page ID or alias (B), and session ID (C).

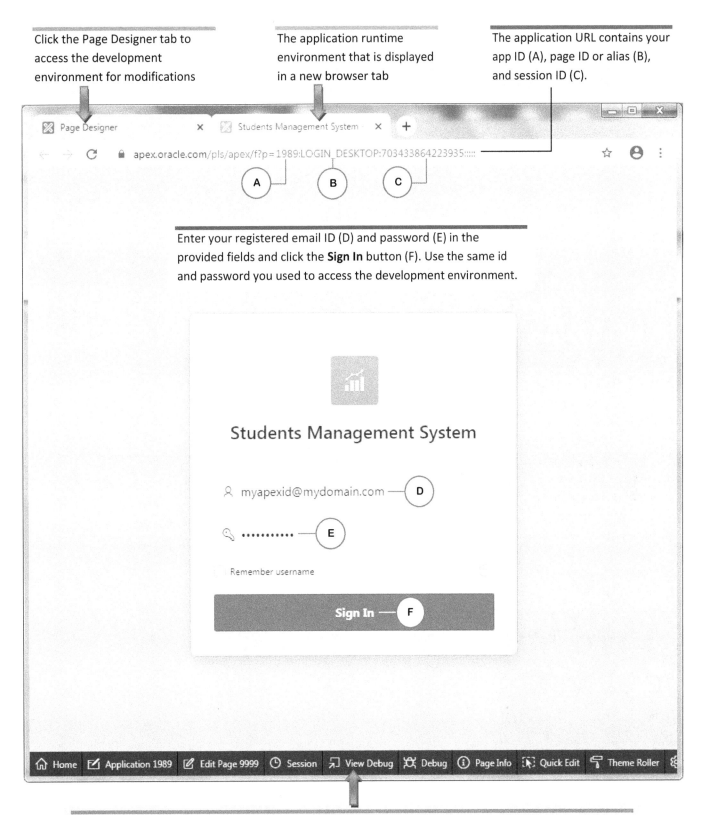

Enter your registered email ID (D) and password (E) in the provided fields and click the **Sign In** button (F). Use the same id and password you used to access the development environment.

When you run an application from Page Designer, the Runtime Developer toolbar appears at the bottom of every editable running page. This toolbar is used to quickly edit the current application or currently running page, view session state, debug information, and apply styles using Theme Roller.

After authenticating the credentials you provided in the Login screen, you are landed on the page you ran in the Page Designer. In the current scenario, you will see Students Report page – Page 2.

This entry in the Navigation bar displays the id of the currently logged in user. The tiny down arrow beside the id has a link to sign out from the application.

This is the application title. You can also set a logo here.

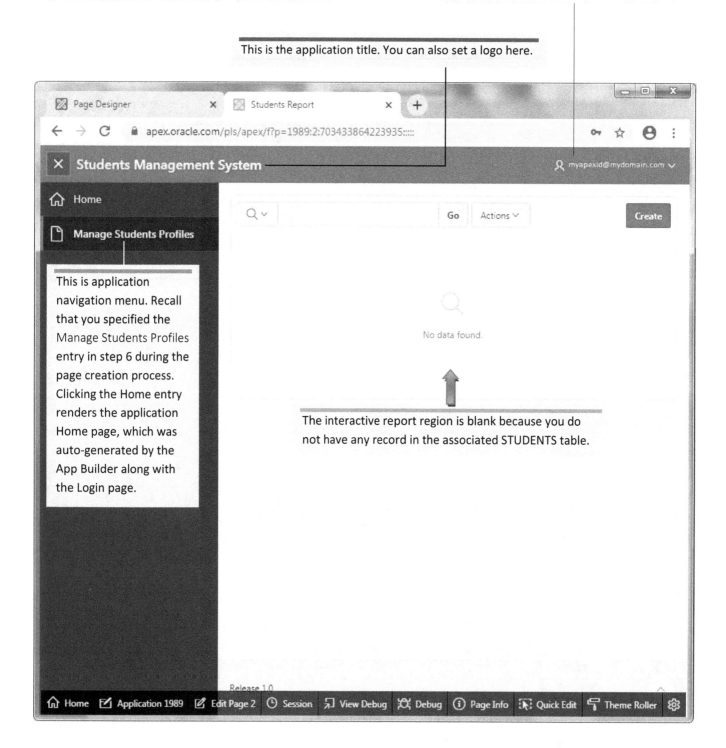

This is application navigation menu. Recall that you specified the Manage Students Profiles entry in step 6 during the page creation process. Clicking the Home entry renders the application Home page, which was auto-generated by the App Builder along with the Login page.

The interactive report region is blank because you do not have any record in the associated STUDENTS table.

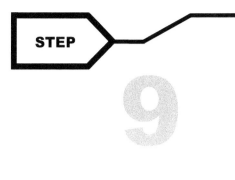

STEP

CREATING RECORD

On Page 2 (Student Report), click the **Create** button (A). The Students Form page (Page 2 - B) will pop up on top of the report page. Enter your name in the Student Name text field (C). Click the calendar icon in the Student DOB field (D), and select your date of birth. Leaving the Student Picture field blank, click the **Create** button (E). The form page will be closed and the report page will be refreshed to display the record (F). Note the auto-generated value in the Student ID primary key column (G), which is generated by the STUDENT_SEQ sequence object – see Section 2.5.1.1 - Specify Primary Key. Mandatory fields in input forms are marked with a tiny red triangle (H). See Chapter 2 Section 2.5.1 & 2.5.1.3 Modify Column.

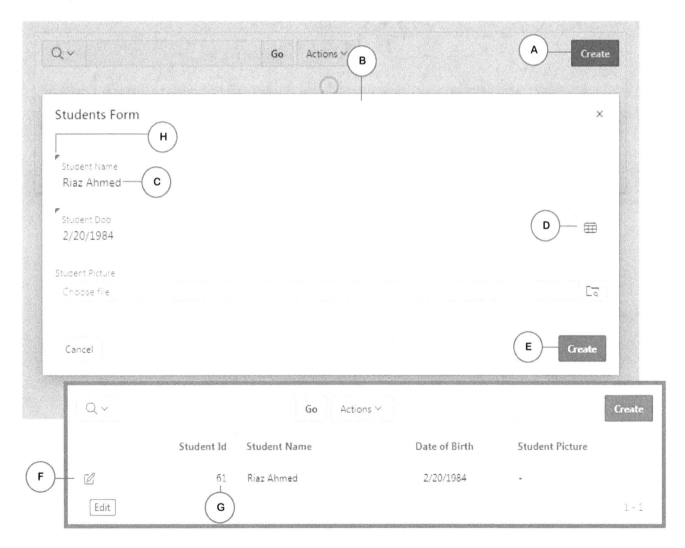

3.4 Examine Database Objects

After creating the first student record through the input form, let's examine the data in the STUDENTS table and examine other relevant database objects (via Object Browser) that are used behind the scene for this process.

1. Select Object Browser from the SQL Workshop menu

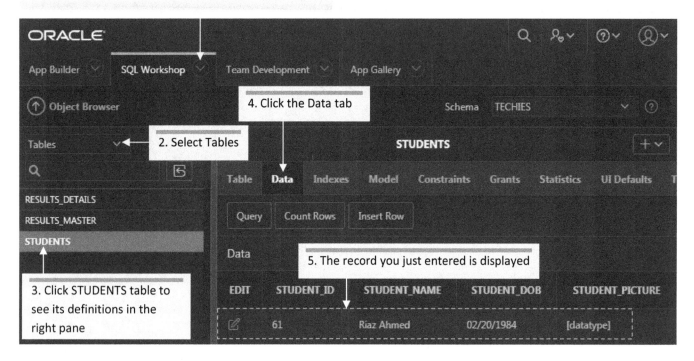

The STUDENT_ID (61) was generated automatically by the following sequence object.

6. Select Sequences from the select list

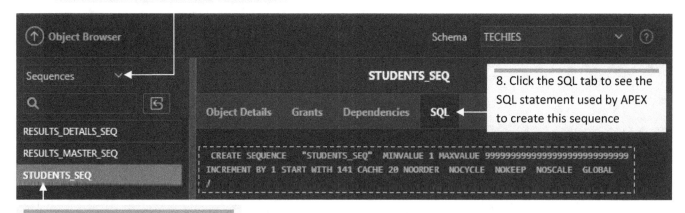

7. Click STUDENTS_SEQ sequence

When you create a new student record, the following trigger (BI_STUDENTS) is fired to obtain a value for the STUDENT_ID column from the STUDENTS_SEQ sequence object. The BI prefix (which stands for Before Insert) denotes that this trigger is fired every time you insert a record in the STUDENTS table.

9. Select Triggers from the select list

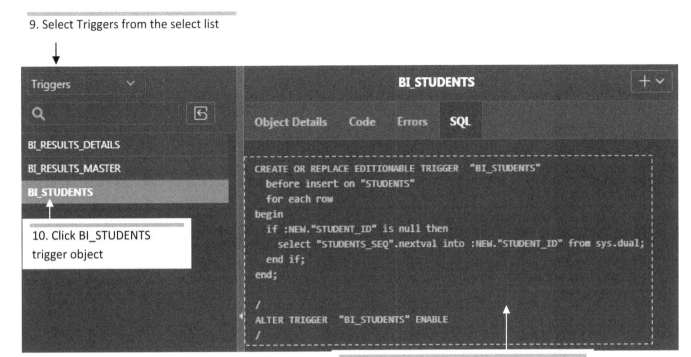

10. Click BI_STUDENTS trigger object

11. Click the SQL tab to see the PL/SQL code, which is used to fetch next STUDENTI_ID value from the STUDENTS_SEQ object

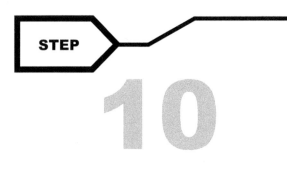

STEP

10

MODIFY/DELETE RECORD

On Page 2 (Student Report), click the **Edit** icon (A). The same form page will pop up again, displaying the selected record (B). Make some changes in both fields and click the **Apply Changes** button (C). The changes will be reflected immediately on the report page. Click the Edit icon again, and delete this record using the Delete button (D). When you click the Delete button, you are prompted with a dialog box (E) to confirm your action.

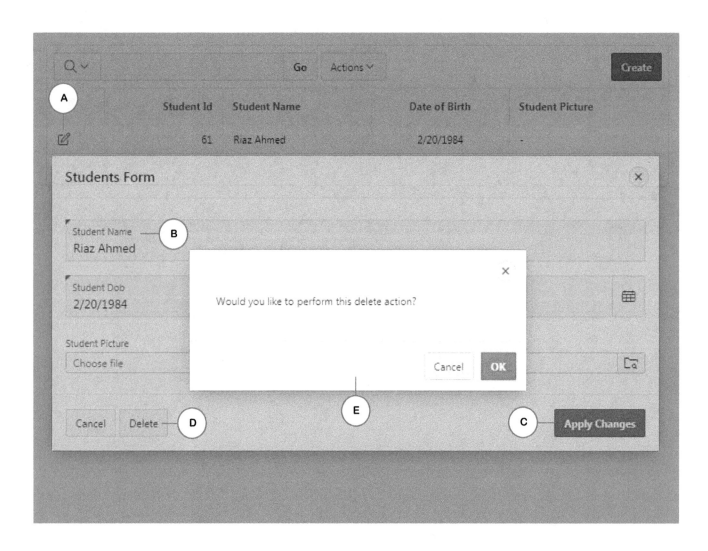

3.5 Page Designer

After experiencing the no-code features of Oracle APEX, let's go through different parts of the Page Designer interface to learn how the whole stuff was generated for us, starting with the Students Report page – Page 2.

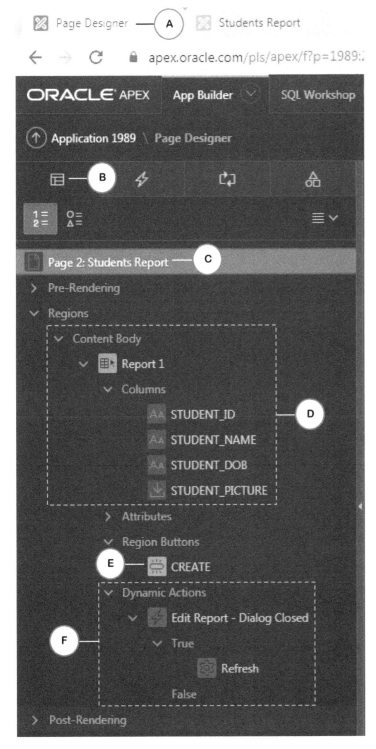

A Click the Page Designer tab in your browser to switch back to the application development mode.

B In the left pane, this is the Rendering tab, which displays regions, page items, buttons, and application logic as nodes in a hierarchical form. The components defined in this section appear on a page when a page is rendered in browser.

C Displays number and name of the currently viewed application page.

D Page components (such as Interactive Report, Interactive Grid, Text Items, Charts, Buttons, and so on) are placed under the *Content Body* node, which comes under the *Regions* node. Here Report 1 is an Interactive Report, you created in step 5. The Columns node under the Report 1 node contains the four columns from the STUDENTS table.

E The CREATE button is placed under the Report 1 region, so at run time it will appear in this region and it is used to call the form page to add records of new students.

F By creating a dynamic action, developers can define complex client-side behavior. This one is an auto-generated DA that refreshes the interactive report (Report 1) when the form page (Page 3 which is a modal dialog) is closed.

This is the middle pane of Page Designer. It has three tabs. The following screenshot displays the most commonly used tab – the Layout tab. The Layout tab is a visual representation of how the components are positioned on the page. By selecting a component and right-clicking, you can delete, move, or copy the component to other regions, or new regions on the page. You can also move existing regions, items, and buttons relative to other components by simply clicking on the component and dragging it to the new location.

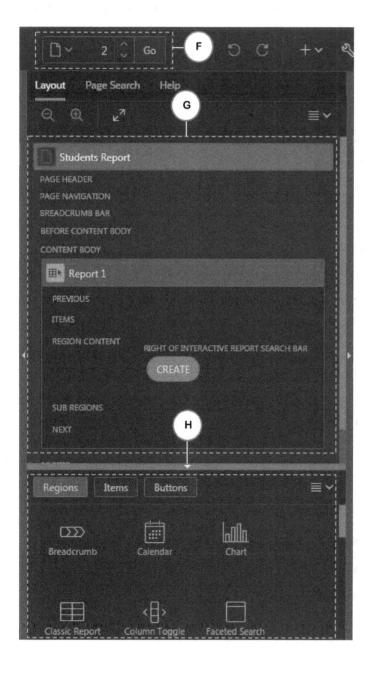

F This is Page Finder which appears on the toolbar. As the name implies, you can use it to find and call an application page in Page Designer. Type the desired page number in the text box and click the Go button, or use the arrow keys to step through application pages.

G The upper section in the middle pane of Page Designer displays a layout of page components used on the current page.

H The lower section in the middle pane contains page components under their respective categories. You can drag and drop a component to a region in the upper section. For example, if you wish to add a chart to your page, drag it from the Regions tab and drop it in the desired region in the upper section.

The right pane in Page Designer is called Property Editor. The Property Editor is used to modify the attributes of the currently selected component. Property Editor displays all attributes for the currently selected component. When you select multiple components (using ctrl+click or shift+click) in the Rendering tab, the Property Editor only displays common attributes. Updating a common attribute updates that attribute for all of the selected components.

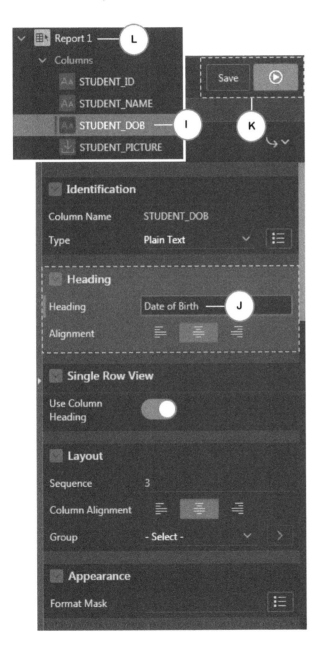

I When you select a component in the Rendering pane on the left side (for example, STUDENT_DOB column), the Property Editor displays its attributes, such as its name, type and more.

J You can change the default attributes of a component (set by the page creation wizard) in the Property Editor. For instance, click the STUDENT_DOB column in the left pane, and change its Heading property from Student_Dob to **Date of Birth**.

K After making any modifications in the Property Editor, you have to click either Save button or Save and Run page button. The Save button makes your modifications permanent, but you stay in the Page Designer interface. The Save and Run page button saves your modifications and runs the page in another browser tab.

L Click Report 1 and have a look at its attributes in the Property Editor. The source of this interactive report in an auto-generated SQL Query, created by the wizard in step 7.

The Form Page: At runtime, you accessed the Form page (Page 3: Students Form) initially via a button (step 9), and then via a link in the Students Report page (step 10). The form page appeared on top of the report page. It contains some input items, and four buttons to perform data manipulation operations.

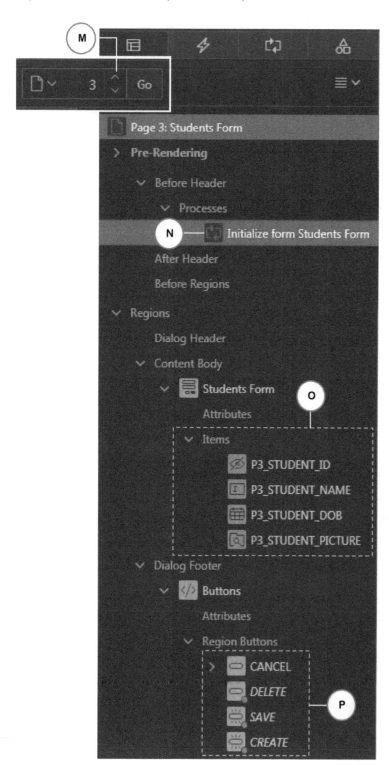

M In the Page Finder section on the toolbar, click the up-arrow icon in the spinner. This will bring up the Students Form page (Page 3) definitions on your screen.

N This process is responsible to initialize form region items. When you click a link in the Students Report page, the process fetches data from the region source, using the primary key value (STUDENT_ID) and displays values in relevant items (O) on the form.

O These page items receive user input for new student's record. When you call an existing record, these items are populated with relevant values from the STUDENT table by the process defined in the previous point. Page items holding primary key values (such as STUDENT_ID) are handled behind the scenes and are thus marked as Hidden items. For example, click the P3_STUDENT_ID item, and have a look at its Type property in the Property Editor.

P These buttons were used to create, modify, delete or cancel a student's record.

Finally, click the Processing tab (A) and expand the Processing node. You will see two processes – Process form Students Form and Close Dialog (B). The first one is an Automatic Row Processing (DML) type process (C), which is responsible to save and delete values to and from the STUDENTS table, respectively. Processes are logic controls used to execute Data Manipulation Language (DML) or PL/SQL. Processes are executed after the page is submitted. A page is typically submitted when a user clicks a button. When you click Create or Apply Changes button on this page, the page is submitted and the first process is executed to save the values you provided on the form in the STUDENTS table. The Close Dialog process (D) is placed in the second position, so it is executed after the first one is executed successfully. The objective of this process is to close the form page.

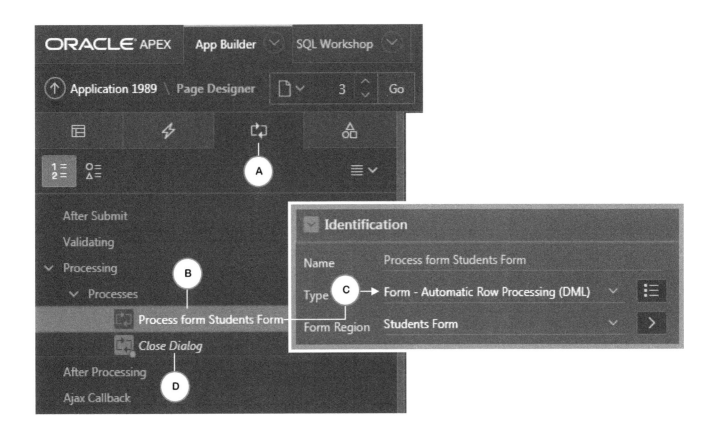

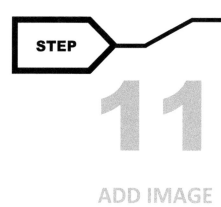

STEP

11

ADD IMAGE

In this step you will add a student's image via the form page. On Page 2 (Student Report), click the Edit icon (A). Then, in the form page, click the folder icon (B) to choose a picture. The Open dialog box will appear. Choose a small image file from your PC, and click the **Open** button. The image file name (C) will appear in the Student Picture field in the Students Form. Click the **Apply Changes** button. The form page will be closed and you will see a Download link in the Student Picture column (D) on the report page. Proceed to the next step to display the image you just uploaded in this column.

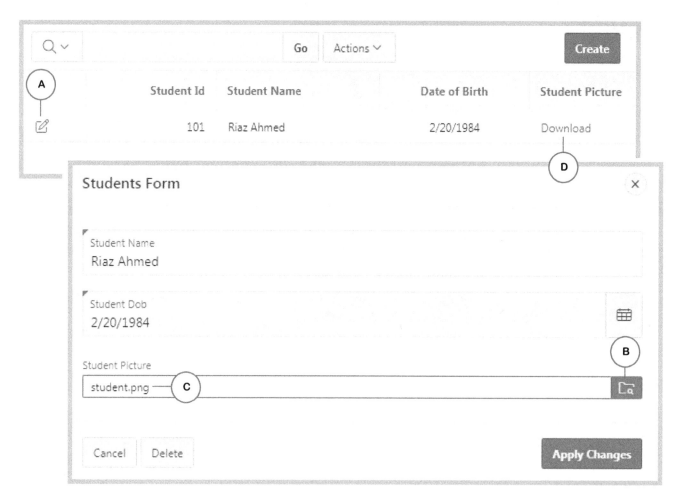

STEP

DISPLAY IMAGE

In your browser, click the **Page Designer** tab (A). Under the Columns node, click the **STUDENT_PICTURE** column (B). The properties of this column will appear in the Property Editor pane (C). Set the Type attribute of this column to **Display Image** (D). Click the **Save and Run Page** button (E). The output of this modification is illustrated on the next page.

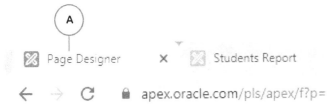

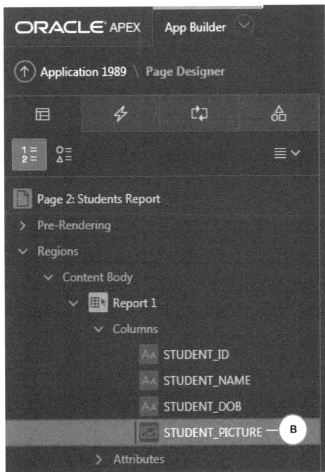

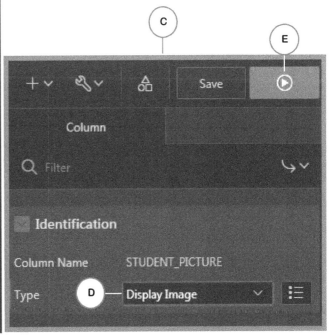

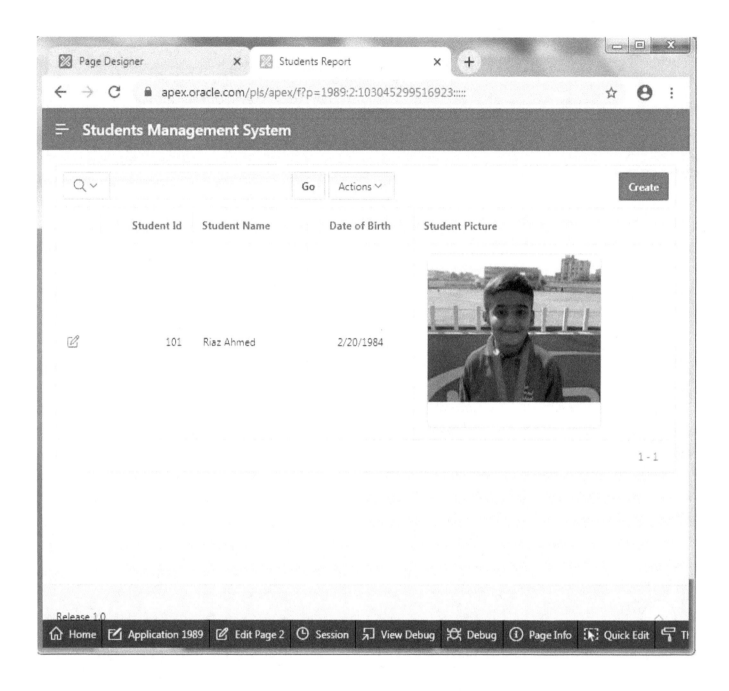

4

Create Master Detail Pages
Without Writing Any Code

4.1 Master Detail Pages

In the previous chapter, you created simple report and input form pages to view and manipulate students' profiles. In this chapter, you will create two more pages with the help of the page creation wizard. These pages will be connected to the RESULTS_MASTER and RESULTS_DETAILS tables (created in chapter 2) to store students' results.

In this chapter, you will create an interactive report page (as you created in the previous chapter) to display header information from the RESULTS_MASTER table, and a Master Detail form. A master detail is a type of page, which reflects a one-to-many relationship between two tables in a database. Master detail pages enable users to insert, update, and delete values from two tables. Typically, a master detail page type displays a master row and multiple detail rows within a single HTML form, as illustrated in the following figure.

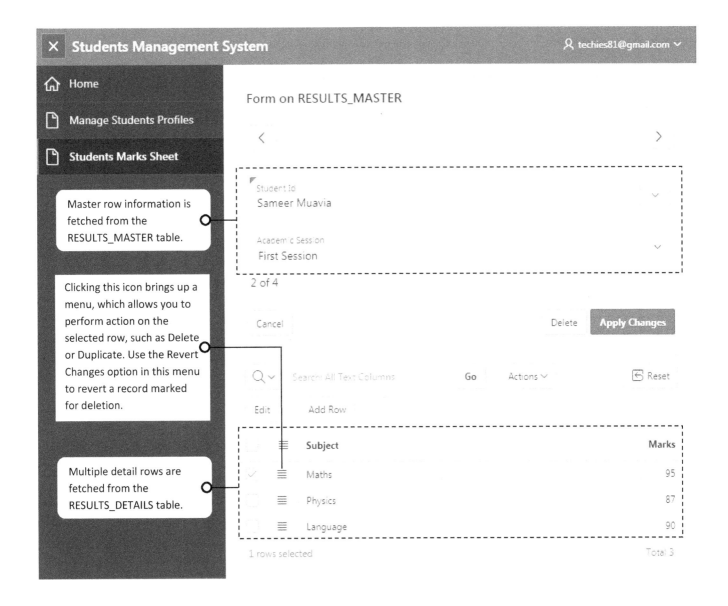

STEP

1

If you are logged off, log back in to the APEX environment using the URL you bookmarked in Chapter 1 – Section 1.6. Open the application by clicking the **edit** icon (A) on the App Builder page. Then, click the **Create Page** button (B).

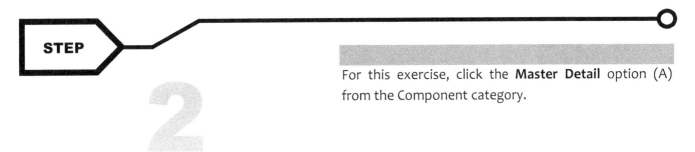

STEP

2

For this exercise, click the **Master Detail** option (A) from the Component category.

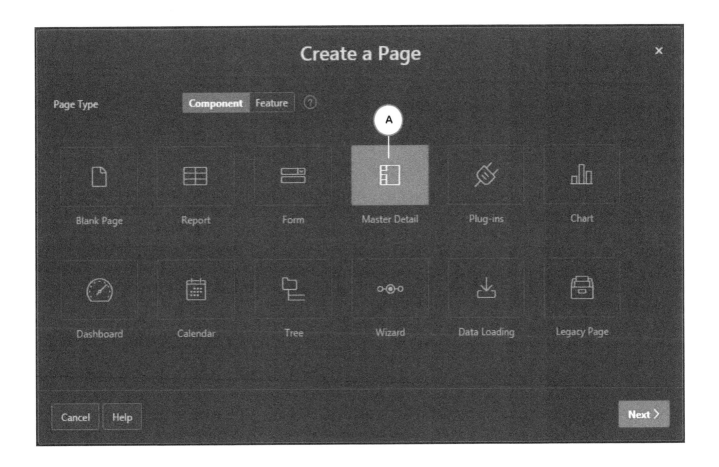

STEP

3

On the next wizard screen, click the **Drill Down** option. A Drill Down master detail contains two pages based on two related tables. The first page contains an interactive report that displays data from the master table. The second page contains two sections – a standard form (to display data from the master table) and an interactive grid (to show information from the details table).

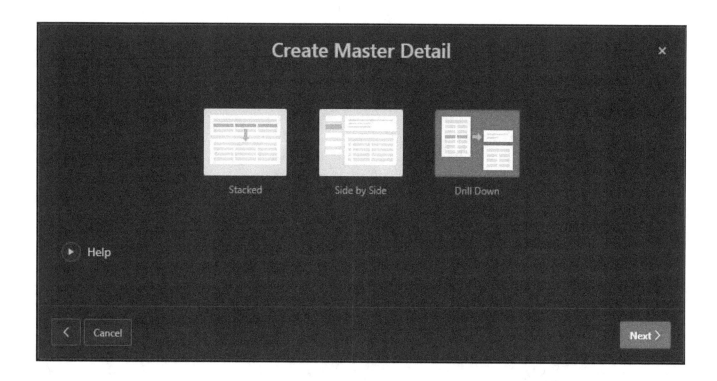

STEP

4

On the *Page Attributes* wizard screen, enter **4** (A) for Master Page Number, and type **Marks Sheet Report** (B) for its name. For Detail Page Number, enter **5** (C), and type **Marks Sheet Form** (D) for its name. As just mentioned the master page (Page 4) will display an interactive report, while the details page (Page 5) will have an input form to receive marks information for each student. Click **Next**.

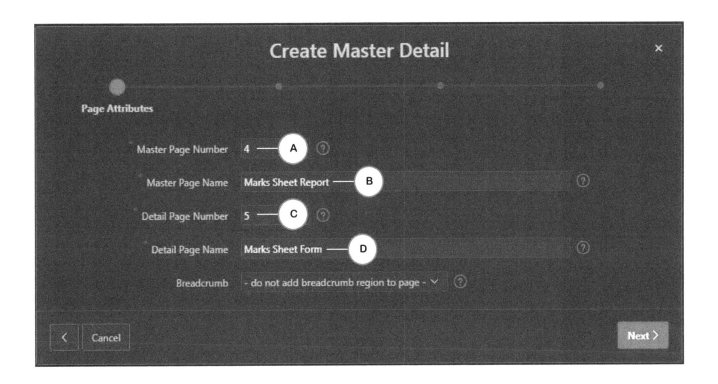

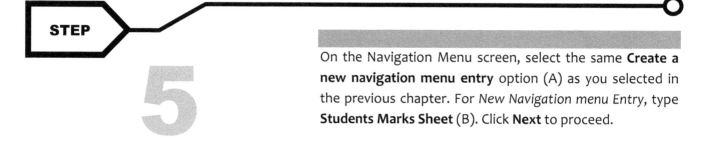

STEP

5

On the Navigation Menu screen, select the same **Create a new navigation menu entry** option (A) as you selected in the previous chapter. For *New Navigation menu Entry*, type **Students Marks Sheet** (B). Click **Next** to proceed.

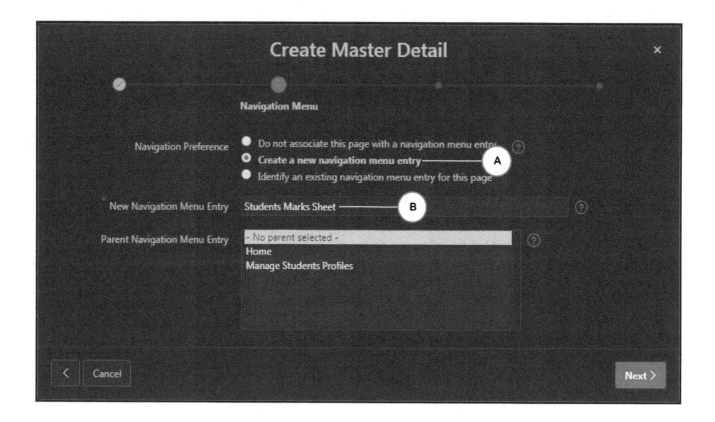

STEP

6

On the Master Source screen, we have to provide master table information. Select **Local Database** (A) for *Location*. Click the popup LOV icon (B), and select the **RESULTS_MASTER** table from the popup list. For the *Primary Key Column*, select **RESULT_ID** (C) from the provided list. All columns from the selected table will appear in the right pane. For *Form Navigation Order*, select the **RESULT_ID** column (D). The form page will provide next and previous buttons for navigation. The values from this column will be used to navigate to a different record. Click **Next**.

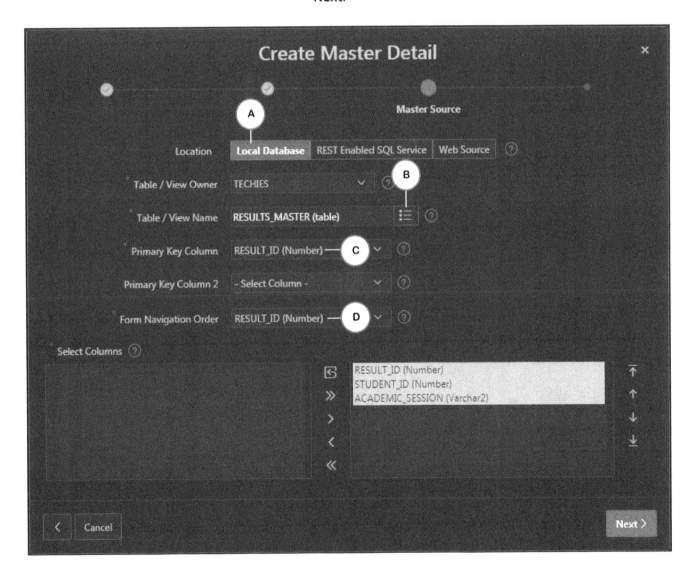

STEP

7

On the final *Detail Source* screen, you specify specs of the details table. Select the **RESULTS_DETAILS** table (A). For Primary Key column, select **LINE_NO** (B). For *Master Detail Foreign Key*, select **RESULT_ID -> RESULT_ID** (C) from the adjacent list. This value specifies the column that creates relationship between the master and detail tables. Recall that both master and detail tables have the RESULT_ID column that creates a relationship between the two tables, and which controls display of correct related detail records during navigation. Click the **Create** button to complete the page creation process.

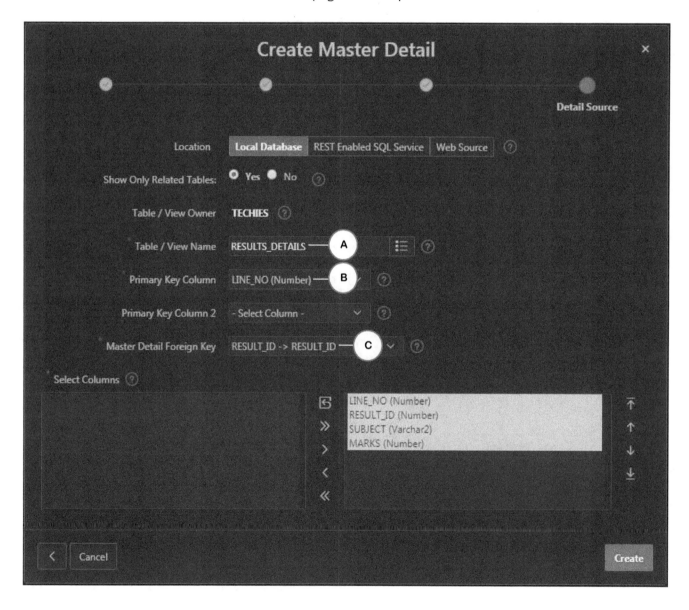

STEP

The last action will land you on Page Designer displaying the interactive report page (Page 4). In Page Finder, click the up arrow icon (A) to fetch Page 5 in the Page Designer. On the Rendering tab in the left pane, click the **Marks Sheet Form** region (B), an interactive grid that allows you to enter details of marks obtained by each student. As you click this region, its properties appear in the Property Editor on the right side. In the Property Editor, scroll down to the Server-side Condition section, and remove the condition (Item is NOT NULL) by choosing - **Select** - (C) for the *Type* property. Click the **Save** button to preserve the change. The default condition you just removed displays the interactive grid only when you modify an existing record. For new, record, it is hidden. By removing the default condition, the interactive grid is displayed to enter marks details.

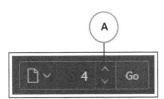

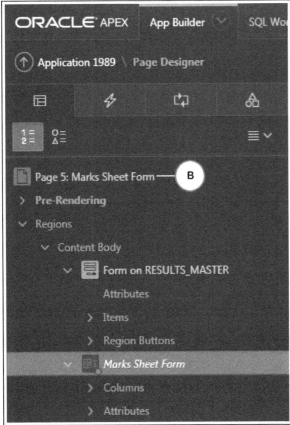

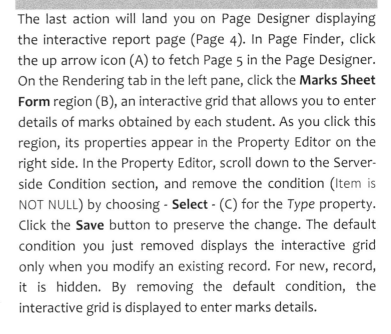

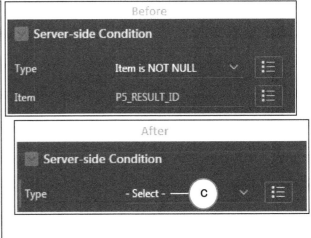

If the application is not running, log in to it. Click the **Students Marks Sheet** option in the main application menu (A). The interactive report page (Page 4) will be rendered. Click the **Create** button (B). The form page (Page 5) will appear on your screen.

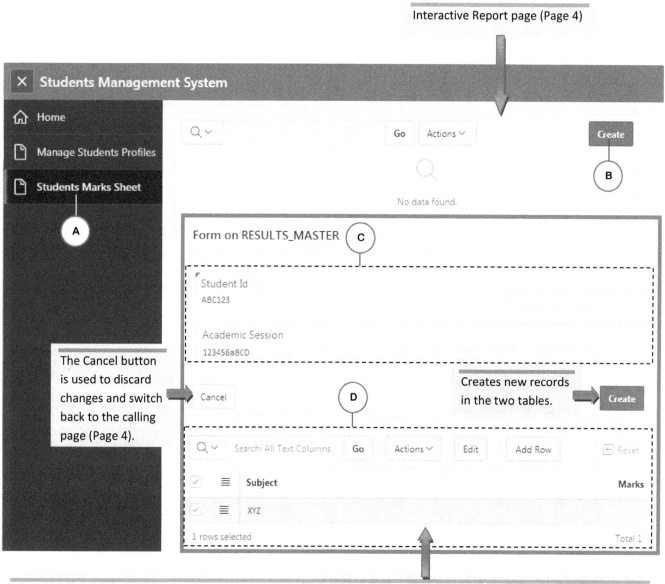

The input form page (Page 5) consists of two sections. The upper section (C) is called master section, which displays information from the RESULTS_MASTER table in the two text boxes. The lower section (D) is an interactive grid, which is just like an Excel sheet. It collects information in multiple rows and columns, and writes this information to the RESULTS_DETAILS table. The Edit and Add Row buttons in the interactive grid region are used to modify and add more information, respectively. Note that there are no items on the page (at run time) for primary and foreign keys from the two database tables. This is because these keys are handled behind the scene by APEX. The only visible foreign key on the page is STUDENT ID, and this is visible because you have to select students manually whose marks you intend to save in the tables. The Student Id is a text field on this page, so you can enter anything in it. Similarly, the Subject column in the interactive grid is also open to receive any text. In order to store valid data in the two tables, you have to restrict users to select valid values and this can be done with the help of some other page components, such as select list or popup list of values.

4.2 Shared Components and List of Values

Shared components are application structures used in APEX application pages. These structures are called shared components because you create them once and utilize them across all the pages in the application. For example, the application menu is a shared component that appears on every application page.

In this chapter, you will create some shared component named List of Values (LOVs). List of values (abbreviated as LOVs) are defined by running the LOV wizard. Once created, LOVs are stored in the List of Values repository and are utilized by page items. You can create two types of LOVs: static and dynamic. A static LOV displays and returns predefined values such as Yes and No, while a dynamic list is populated using values from database tables or some other dynamic source. After creating an LOV you associate it to page items such as select list, popup LOV, radio group, checkbox, and so on.

STEP

9

In the following steps, you will create one dynamic and two static LOVs via Shared Components interface. Using these LOVs users will be able to select and store valid data. On the main application page, click the icon labeled **Shared Components** (A). The Shared Components page, as illustrated on the next page, should come up.

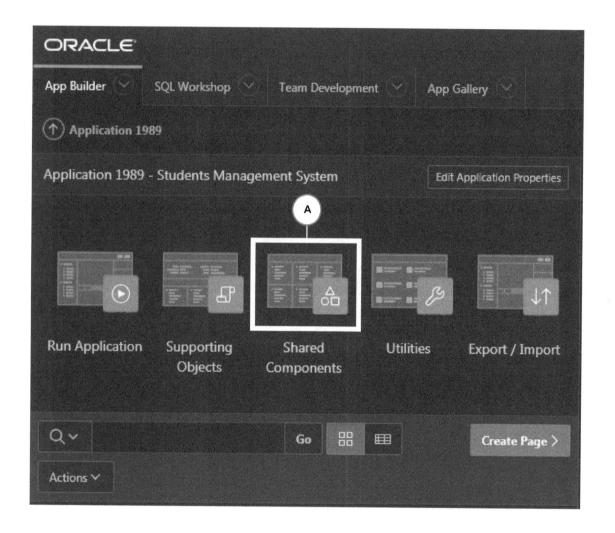

STEP

10

The Shared Components page has multiple sections. Each section contains multiple options that help you create different types of components. Once you create a component, you can utilize it in your application as many times as you want. In the Shared Components page (A), click the **List of Values** link (B). In the Lists of Values page (C), click the **Create** button (D).

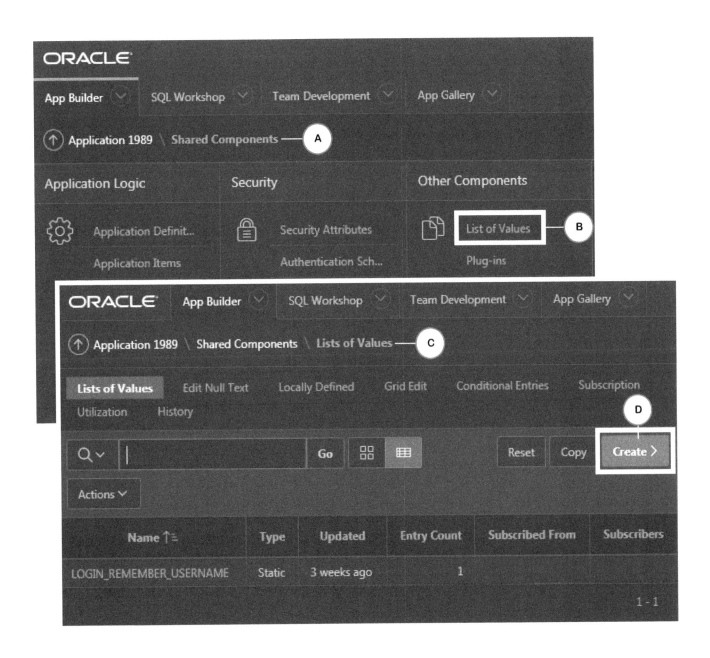

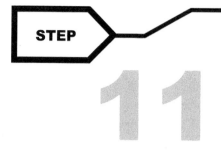

STEP

On the Source wizard screen, select the **From Scratch** option (A), and click **Next**. On the Name and Type screen, enter **STUDENTS_LOV** (B) for the LOV name, and set its type to **Dynamic** (C). Click **Next** to proceed. As mentioned earlier, a dynamic list is populated using values from database tables or some other dynamic source.

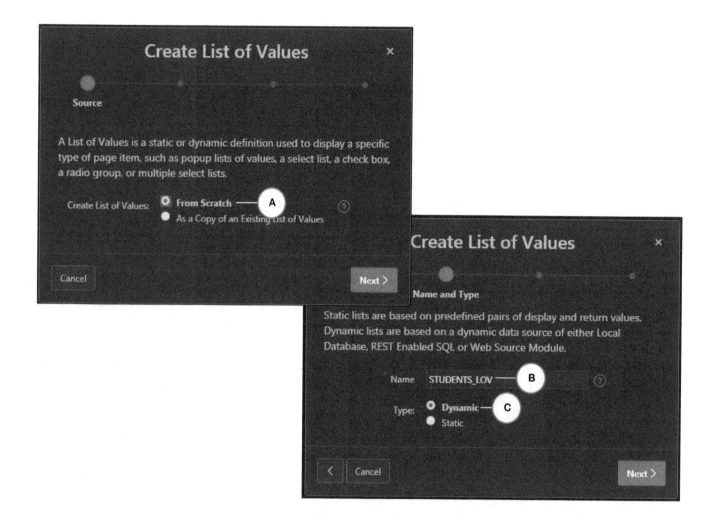

STEP

12

For Data Source, select **Local Database** (A), and for Source Type, select the **Table** option (B). The Table/View Owner displays the Oracle database schema you are connected to. This is the schema where all your database objects reside. From the Table/View Name list, choose the **STUDENTS** table (C), and click **Next**. These selections specify that you want to create a dynamic LOV on the STUDENTS table, which is a table in the local database. On the Column Mappings screen, select **STUDENT_ID** (D) for Return Column, and **STUDENT_NAME** (E) for Display Column. Click **Create** (F) to complete the LOV creation process.

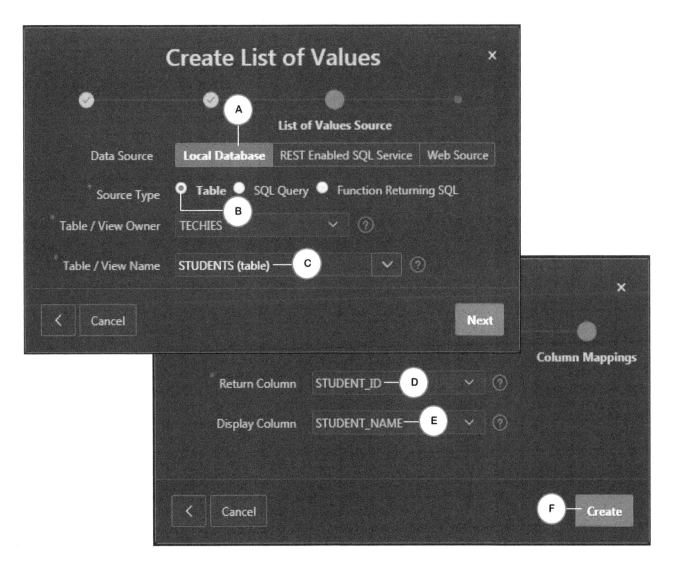

STEP

13

In the remaining steps you will associate the STUDENTS LOV to the STUDENT_ID field on Page5 – Marks Sheet Form. After clicking the Create button in the last step, the STUDENTS LOV will be displayed on the Lists of Values page (A). Click the application id link (B) in the breadcrumb list to access the main application page (C). On this page, click the **Page 5** icon (D) to open this page in Page Designer.

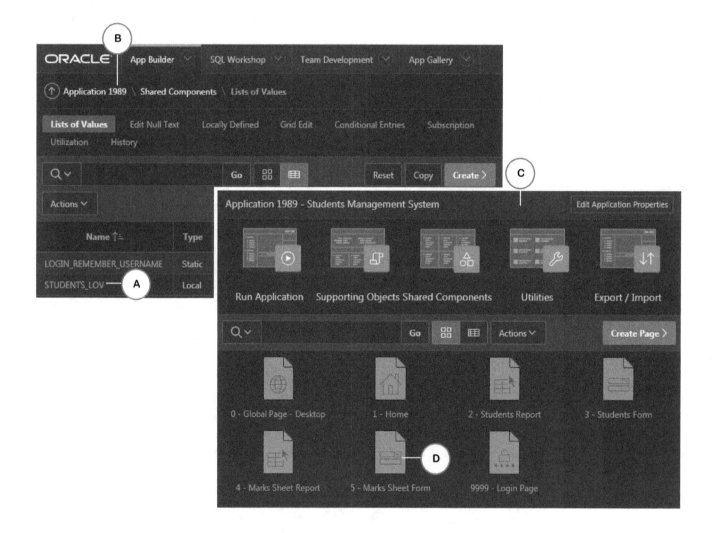

STEP

14

With Page 5 displaying on your screen, expand the Items node (A) under the Form on RESULTS_MASTER region, and click the **P5_SUTDENT_ID** item (B). In the Identification section in Property Editor, change the type of this item from Number Field to **Popup LOV** (C). Scroll down to the List of Values section, set the type of LOV to **Shared Components** (D), and select the **STUDENTS_LOV** (E) for the List of Values property. Click the **Save and Run Page** button (F). The output of this association is illustrated on the next page.

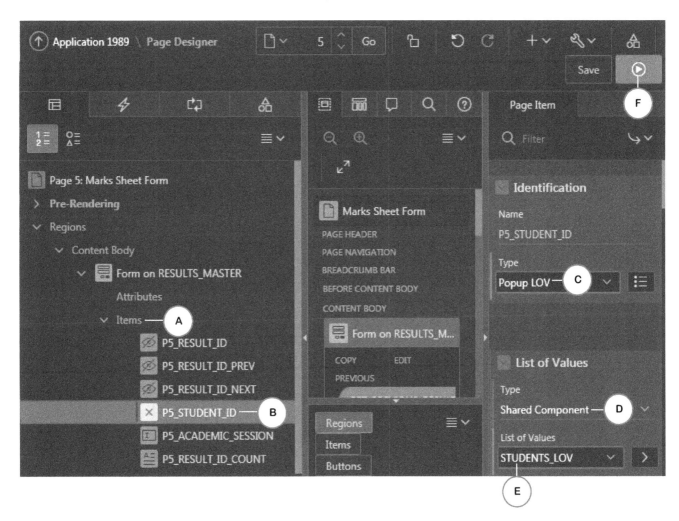

Click the arrow icon to see a list of existing students from the STUDENTS table. The list ensures that users select a valid predefined value.

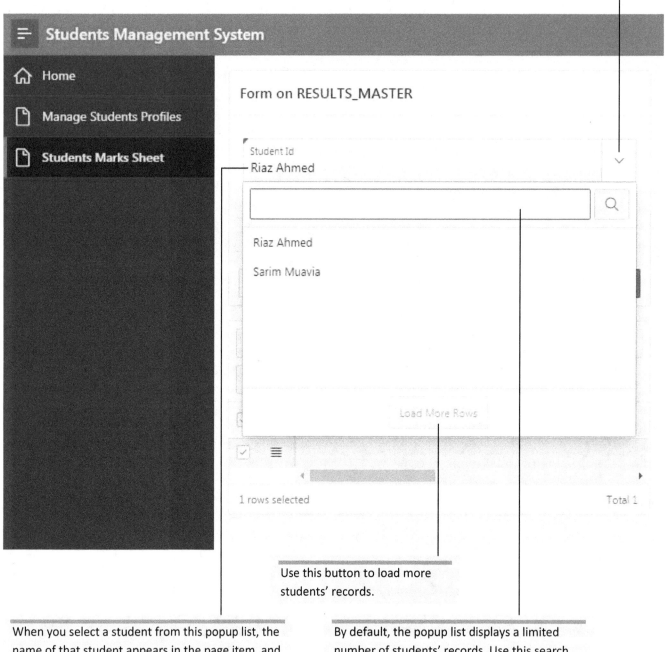

Use this button to load more students' records.

When you select a student from this popup list, the name of that student appears in the page item, and his/her id is stored in the background for internal processing.

By default, the popup list displays a limited number of students' records. Use this search box to locate a student (by name) who is not visible in the list.

STEP

15

In these steps, you will create a couple of static LOVs. These LOVs will be used to select academic sessions and subjects. If you've exited the Shared Components page, access it and click the **List of Values** link as mentioned in Step 9 and 10. Create a new LOV from scratch (Step 11). On the Name and Type wizard screen, enter **ACADEMIC_SESSIONS** (A) for the LOV name, and select **Static** (B) as the LOV Type. Click **Next** (C). On the Static Values screen, enter **First Session** (D) in the first Display Value text field, and enter **2020-21** (E) for its Return Value. On the second row, enter **Second Session** (F) as Display Value, and **2021-22** (G) as its Return Value. Click the **Create List of Values** button (H) to complete the process.

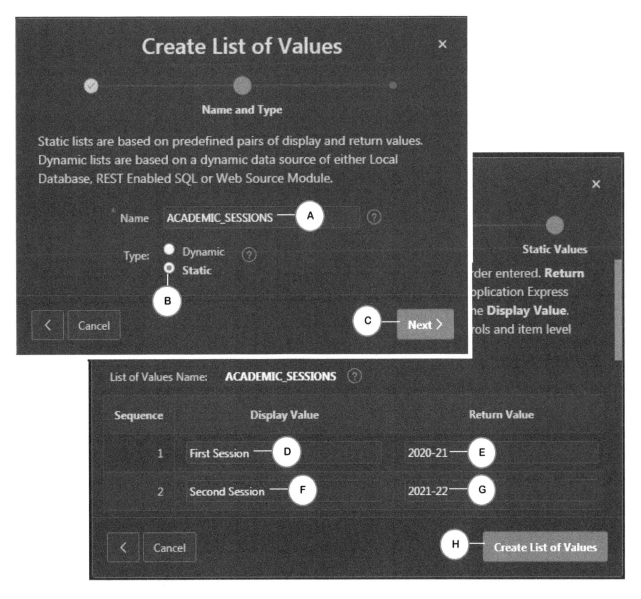

STEP

16

Associate the LOV to the corresponding page item. Expand the Items node (A) under the Form on RESULTS_MASTER region, and click the **P5_ACADEMIC_SESSION** item (B). In the Identification section, change the type of this item to **Select List** (C). Scroll down to the List of Values section, set the type of LOV to **Shared Components** (D), and select the **ACADEMIC_SESSIONS** LOV (E) for the List of Values property. Click the **Save and Run Page** button (F). The output of this association is illustrated on the next page.

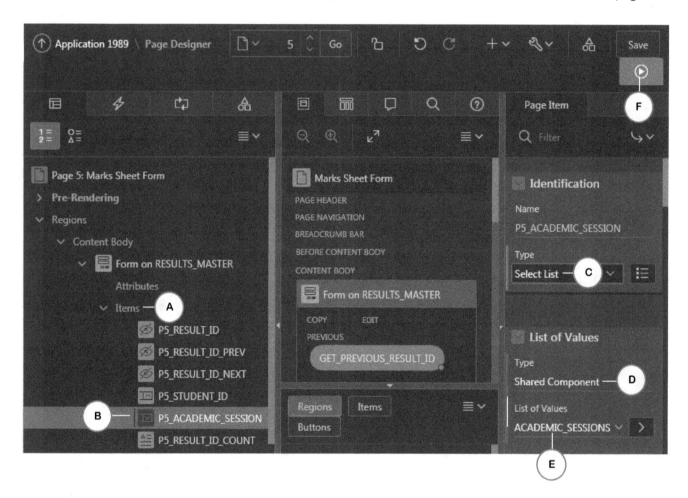

Click the arrow icon to see the list of academic sessions you just created.

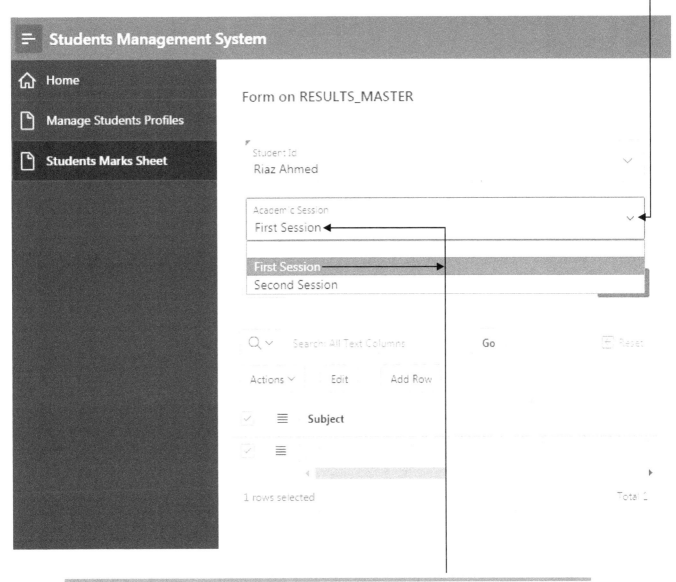

When you select a session from the Select List, the Display Value appears in the Academic Session field, and the Return Value is held in the background for further processing. For example, if you select the First Session display value, then its return value (i.e. 2020-21) is stored in memory. When you save this record, the return value is retrieved from memory and then stored in the ACADEMIC_SESSION column in the RESULTS_MASTER table. You'll see this process in a minute.

STEP

Using the instructions provided in step 15 and 16, create one more static LOV. This LOV will display and return subjects. On the Name and Type wizard screen, enter **SUBJECTS** (A) for the LOV name, and select **Static** (B) as the LOV Type. Click **Next**. On the Static Values screen, enter **Maths**, **Physics**, and **Language** (C) in the Display Value column. Enter the same values in the Return Value column (D). Click the **Create List of Values** button (H) to complete the process. This LOV will return the same value as it displays.

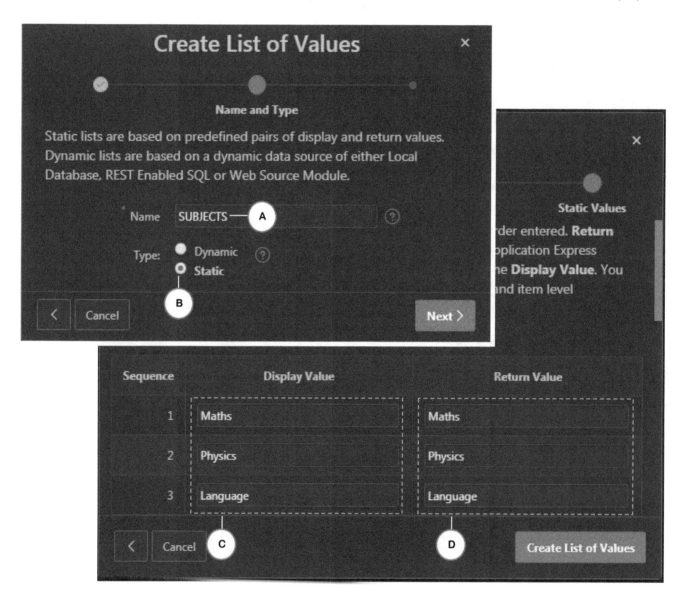

STEP

18

Execute this step to associate the SUBJECTS LOV to the SUBJECT column in the interactive grid on Page 5. Expand the **Columns** node (A) under the Marks Sheet Form interactive grid region. Click the **SUBJECT** column (B). Change the column's Type to **Select List** (C). In List of Values section, once again set Type to **Shared Components** (D), and List of Values to **SUBJECTS** (E). Save and run the page.

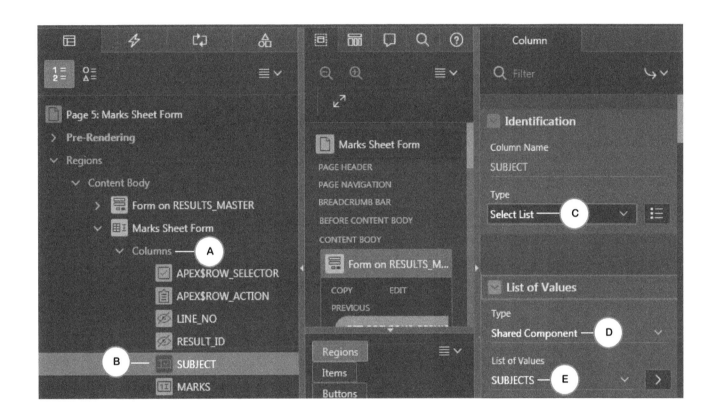

STEP

19

Enter marks information, as illustrated in the following figure. Select a student from the Student Id popup LOV (A). Select an academic session from the corresponding Select List (B). Click the **Create** button (C). The record will be created in the RESULTS_MASTER table, and will be displayed on the Interactive Report page (Page 4) (D). Click the Edit icon (E) to add subjects and marks information for this record. Click the Edit button (F) to activate the interactive grid. Select subjects from the Subject list (G), and provide marks in the Marks column (H). After entering marks for the first subject, use the Add Row button (I) to add more rows to the grid. After providing marks for all three subjects, click the **Apply Changes** button. Add few more records for other students and also try to Delete some of them. The Previous and Next buttons (J) are used for record navigation, and appear on the page only when you have at least two records.

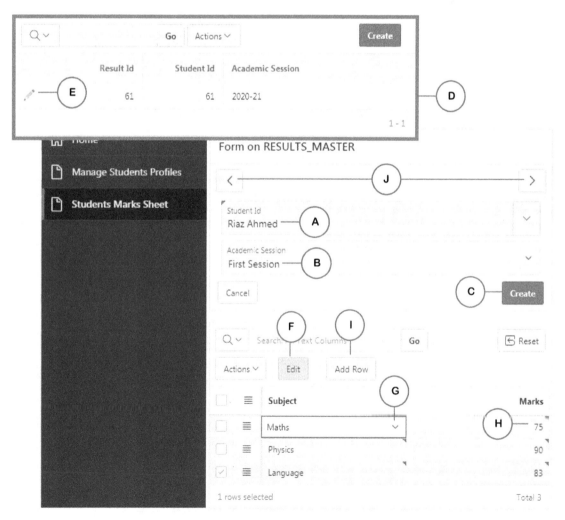

STEP

20

The Student Id column in the interactive report on Page 4 displays numeric id of students. Execute this step to display their names instead of ids. Open **Page 4** (A) in Page Designer. Click the **STUDENT_ID** column (B). Set the Type of this column to **Plain Text (based on List of Value)** (C). For List of Values, select the **STUDENTS_LOV** (D). You used this LOV in step 14 as well. This is the beauty of creating shared components – you create them once and utilize them multiple times in your app. Enter **Student** (E) for Heading, and set Heading and Column alignments to left (F). Save and run this page. Now the students' names (G) will be displayed in the interactive report instead of ids.

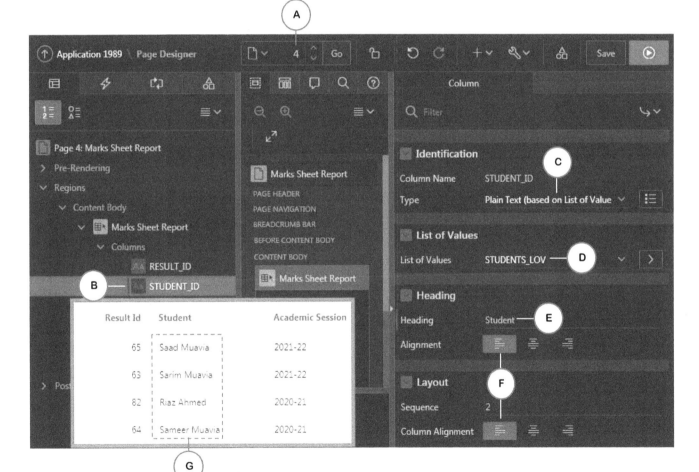

4.3 Anatomy of Pages and Data

Let's go through some important segments of the two pages you created in this chapter.

The Marks Sheet Report page (Page 4) is similar to the Students Report page (Page 2). It also carries an interactive report region (Marks Sheet Report) (A) to display information from the RESULTS_MASTER table. It also has the CREATE button (B), which is used to add new records. Click this button and have a look at its Behavior section in the Property Editor pane.

The Action property is set to Redirect to Page in this Application (C). The Target property (D) is an associated property, where APEX set the target page (Page 5 - Marks Sheet Form) (E) for you. When the CREATE button is clicked, you are redirected to Page 5.

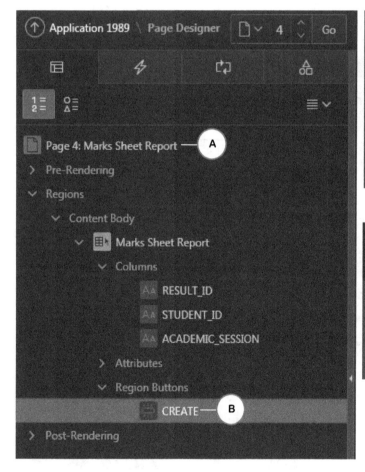

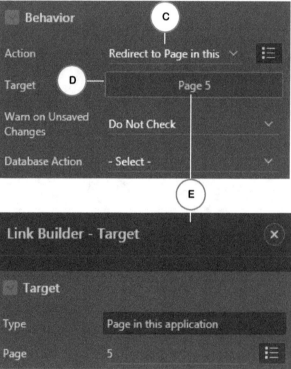

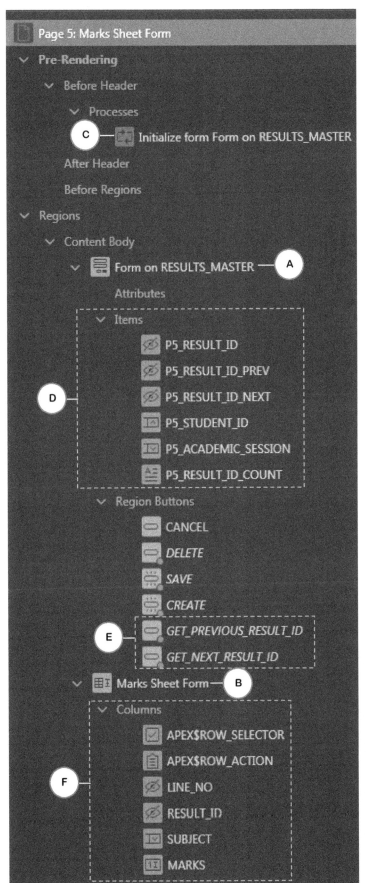

The Marks Sheet Form page (Page 5) comprises two regions – Form on RESULTS_MASTER (A) and Marks Sheet Form (B). The former carries page items (hidden fields and LOVs), while the later region is an interactive grid that accepts subjects and marks information.

C This is the same process you saw in the Students setup module. It is responsible to initialize form region items. When you click a link on the report page (Page 4), the process fetches data from the region source, using the primary key value (RESULT_ID) and displays values in relevant items (D) on the form.

D These page items receive user input for new record. When you call an existing record, these items are populated with relevant values from the RESULTS_MASTER table by the process defined in the previous point. Page items holding primary key values (such as P5_RESULT_ID) are handled behind the scenes and are thus marked as Hidden items. Click the P5_RESULT_ID item, and have a look at its Type property in the Property Editor.

E These buttons were used for navigation – see step 19-J.

F The interactive grid displays columns from the RESULTS_DETAILS table.

The Processing node of Page 5 is revealed in the following figure. The first process (A) handles data of the form region and writes this data to the RESULTS_MASTER table, while the second process (B) handles interactive grid data, which goes into the RESULTS_DETAILS table. Branches enable you to create logic controls that determine how the user navigates through the application. The page contains three branches.

The first two branches (Go To Page 5 - C) are associated with Next and Previous buttons (D) to control navigation. When you navigate among records using the two buttons, these two branches keep you on Page 5. The last one (Go To Page 4) is not associated with any button, so when you click any other button on the page, you are taken back to Page 4. For example, if you click the Apply Changes button, this page is closed and you see Page 4 on your screen.

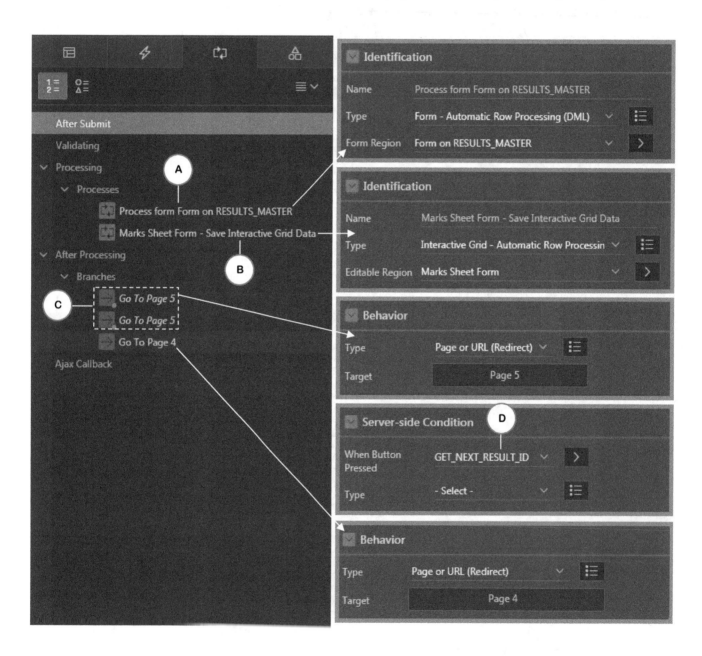

The following figure displays the data stored in the RESULTS_MASTER and RESULTS_DETAILS tables. The RESULTS_MASTER table holds header information – RESULT_ID, STUDENT_ID, and ACADEMIC_SESSION. The RESULTS_DETAILS table stores details information for each RESULT_ID.

For example, the RESULT_ID 82 (A) in the master table has three corresponding records (B) in the details table. The two tables are linked together via the RESULT_ID column, which exists in both tables (C). When you click the edit link on Page 4, APEX uses the RESULT_ID value to display exact records from both tables on Page 5.

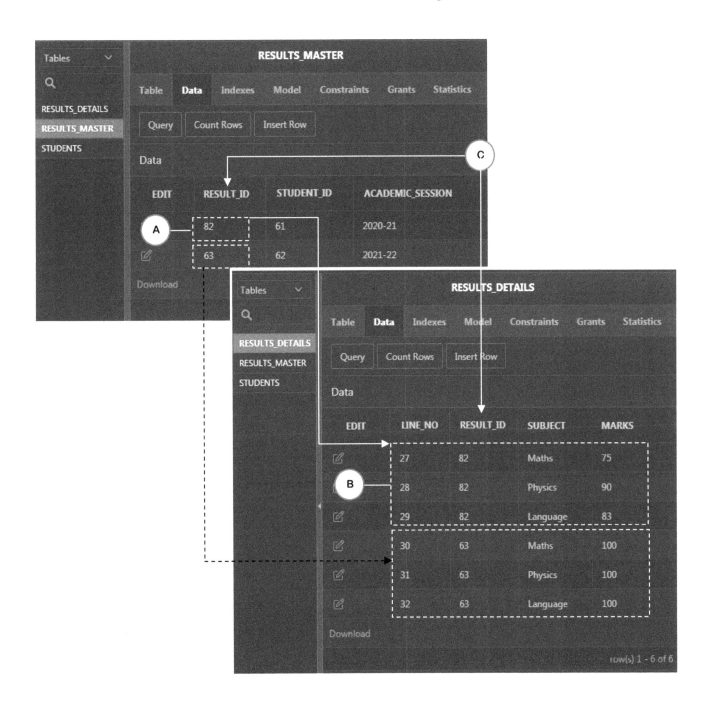

4.4 The Actions Menu

End users use the Actions menu to customize an interactive report. The Actions menu is also available for interactive grid with relevant options. Users can lock, hide, filter, freeze, highlight, and sort data using the Actions menu. They can also define breaks, aggregations, and computations against columns. In this section you will get hands-on exposure to some of these options.

Interactive reports include a search bar at the top of the page which includes the following controls: a columns search icon (A), Text area (B), Go button (C), and Actions menu (D). If I type any part of my name and click the Go button, the report will fetch my record.

Note: Always save interactive report and interactive grid after you do any modification through the Actions menu. See Save Report later in this section.

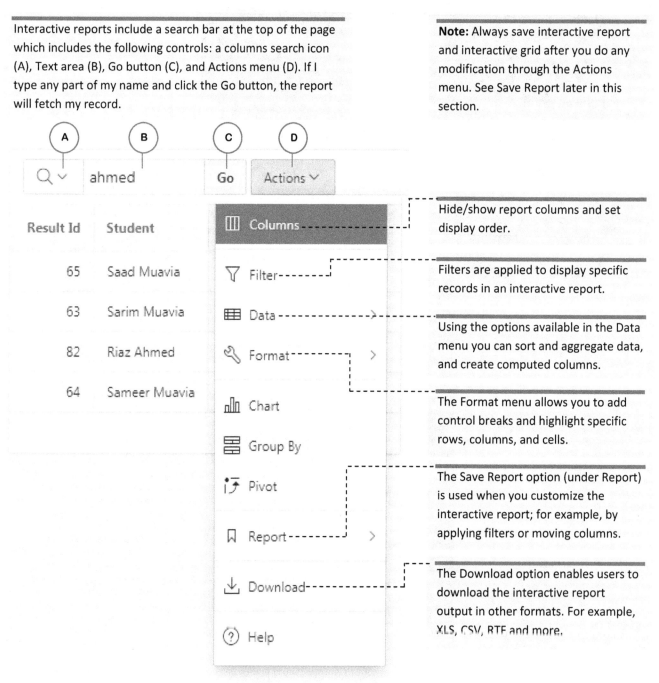

Hide/show report columns and set display order.

Filters are applied to display specific records in an interactive report.

Using the options available in the Data menu you can sort and aggregate data, and create computed columns.

The Format menu allows you to add control breaks and highlight specific rows, columns, and cells.

The Save Report option (under Report) is used when you customize the interactive report; for example, by applying filters or moving columns.

The Download option enables users to download the interactive report output in other formats. For example, XLS, CSV, RTF and more.

COLUMNS

The Columns option in the Actions menu is used to hide and show report columns and to set display order. For example, move the **Result Id** column from Display in Report pane to Do Not Display pane using the left arrow icon (A), and click the Apply button. The column will disappear from the interactive report. To bring it back, move it back to the Display in Report pane using the right Arrow icon.

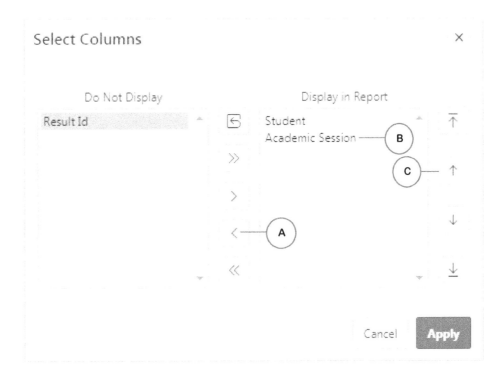

The four buttons on the right side of this dialog are used to alter display sequence of columns in interactive report. For example, click the **Academic Session** column (B) and then click the up arrow icon (C). **Apply** the change. This column will become the first column in your report.

FILTER

Using the Filter option in the Actions menu you can restrict an interactive report to display specific records. On the Filter form (A), you can set Column and Row filters. If you want to apply filter on a column, you have to select the Column tab (B). For example, if you want to see records pertaining to academic session 2020-21, then select this column from the Column list (C), set Operator to '=' (D), select 2020-21 (E) from the Expression list, and click Apply. The applied filter appears between the search bar and the report (F). The interactive report will be filtered to display only the desired records (G).

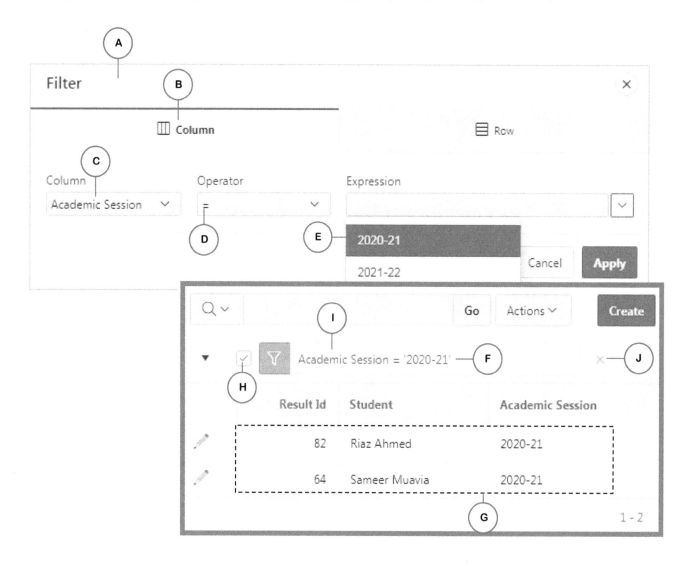

To enable and disable a filter, select and deselect the check box (H) to the left of the filter name. To edit a filter, click the filter name (I). To remove a filter, select the Remove Filter icon (J). Note that you can define multiple filters on a single interactive report. By default, multiple filters display horizontally stacked on top of one another.

SORT

The Sort option is located under the Data menu. The Sort dialog box allows you to sort an interactive report on multiple columns. Just select the desired column(s) and click the Apply button. You can sort the report in Ascending or Descending order using the appropriate option from the Direction list. For example, select the Student column (A) and click Apply (B). The interactive report will be ordered alphabetically by student names. An icon (C) will be placed next to the column heading to signify the sort order. Click this icon to see a small menu and change the sorting order by clicking descending option (D).

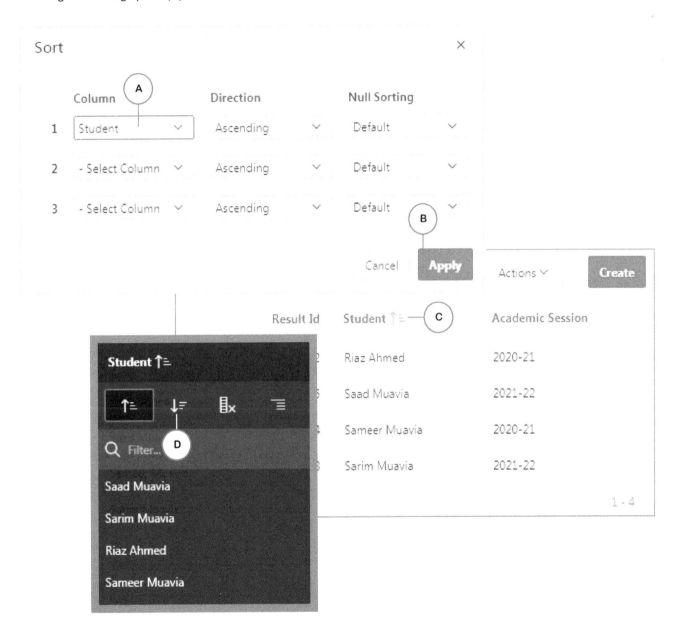

AGGREGATE

The Aggregate option which is also located under the Data menu enables you to display sum of numeric column values. In addition to the Sum function, you also have Count, Average and some other functions to utilize in your interactive report and interactive grid. The best place to test this option is the interactive grid on Page 5. Modify a record on Page 4 to call Page 5. From the Actions menu in the interactive grid, select Aggregate from the Data menu. In the Aggregation dialog box, select Marks (A) from the Column list, set Aggregation to Sum (B), and click Save (C). The sum of Marks (D) will appear at the report bottom. You can modify an existing aggregate by clicking its name (E). Use the plus and minus icons (F) to add and remove functions. To remove a function, first select it by clicking its entry in the above list and then click the minus icon. The Enabled checkbox (G) can be used to enable or disable a function.

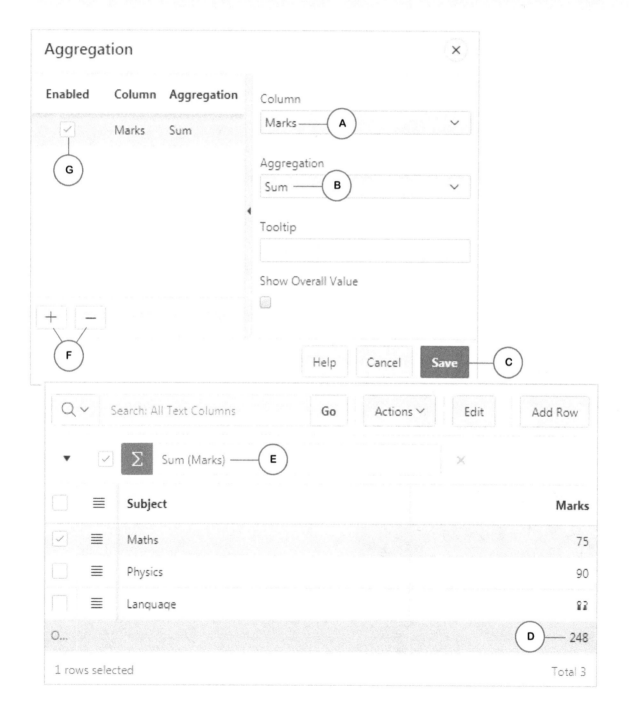

CONTROL BREAK

The Control Break feature (under the Format menu) enables grouping to be added to your report on one or more columns. The Column attribute (A) defines which column to group on and the Status attribute (B) determines whether the control break is active. Select Academic Session (C) and click Apply. You will see that the report results are grouped by the selected column (D) and the Control Break column rule (E) is listed under the toolbar. A checkbox (F) is displayed in front of the Control Break column and is used to turn the control break on or off. The control break can be deleted from the report by clicking the remove icon (G).

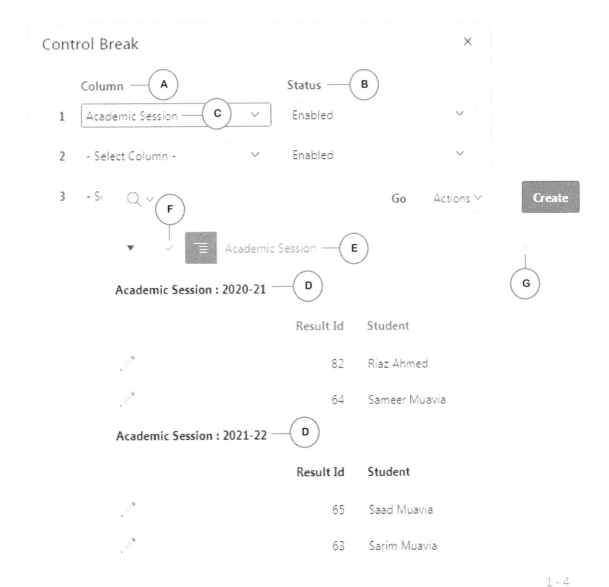

HIGHLIGHT

The highlight feature in Interactive Reports enables users to display data in different colors based on a condition. You can define multiple highlight conditions for a report. In this exercise, you're highlighting a student's record whose name is Sarim Muavia with yellow background and red text color. Since you set the Highlight Type to Row, the condition will apply to the whole record. If you set the Highlight Type to Cell, only the student name will be highlighted.

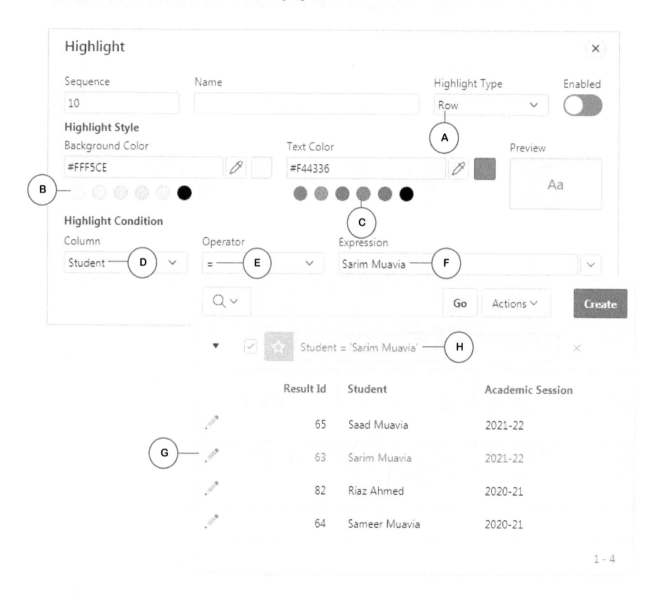

Click Actions | Format | Highlight. Set Highlight Type to Row (A), click the yellow circle (B) for Background Color, and click the red circle (C) for Text Color. In Highlight Condition, select Student (D) from the Column list, select '=' (E) as the operator, enter student's name (F) in Expression box and click Apply. The student's record will be highlighted (G). Modify the highlight rule by clicking its link (H), change the Highlight Type (A) to Cell, and click Apply. Now only the cell containing the student name will be highlighted.

SAVE REPORT

Click the Actions menu again and select Save Report (under Report). From the Save drop-down list, select As Default Report Settings (A). Set Default Report Type to Primary (B) and click Apply. After modifying an interactive report you must save it using this procedure, otherwise you'll lose the applied settings when you exit the application (without saving the report) and access it later.

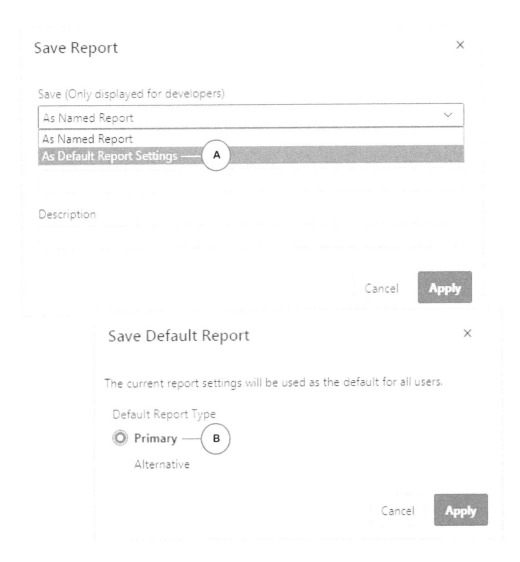

DOWNLOAD

The Download option enables you to download an interactive report as a comma-delimited file (CSV) format, HTML, Microsoft Excel (XLS) format, Adobe Portable Document Format (PDF), Microsoft Word Rich Text Format (RTF), or as HTML attached to an email. Click the Email option (A). Enter your email address in the To box (B), and click Send (C). After a while, you will receive an email (D) in your email account, carrying an html attachment (E).

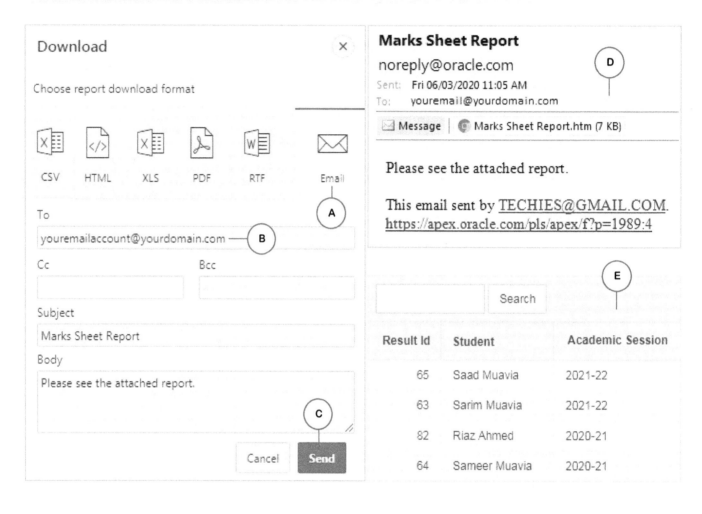

5

Create No-Code Application From Microsoft Excel File

5.1 Creating App from a File

In the previous chapters you executed steps to create a conventional APEX web application, its database objects, and pages. In this chapter you will use an alternate method of creating app using an MS Excel file. The file contains data about books available on Amazon.

The web application (as illustrated in the following figure) and its backend database table will be created using books.xlsx file. The file is available in the downloaded source – see *About this book* section at the beginning of this book. The file contains information, such as book title, ISBN, book image path, author, genre, publishing date, and price.

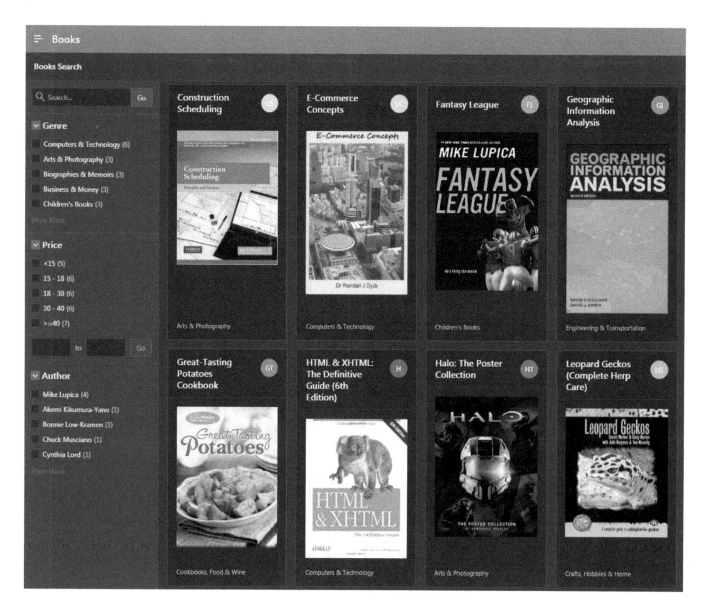

After downloading the book.xlsx file, execute the following set of steps to create the application. Log in to Oracle APEX development environment – see Chapter 1 Section 1.6.

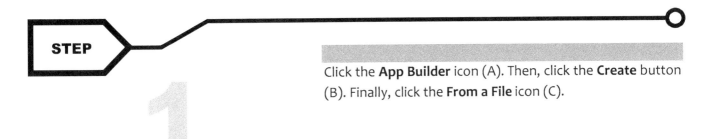

STEP

Click the **App Builder** icon (A). Then, click the **Create** button (B). Finally, click the **From a File** icon (C).

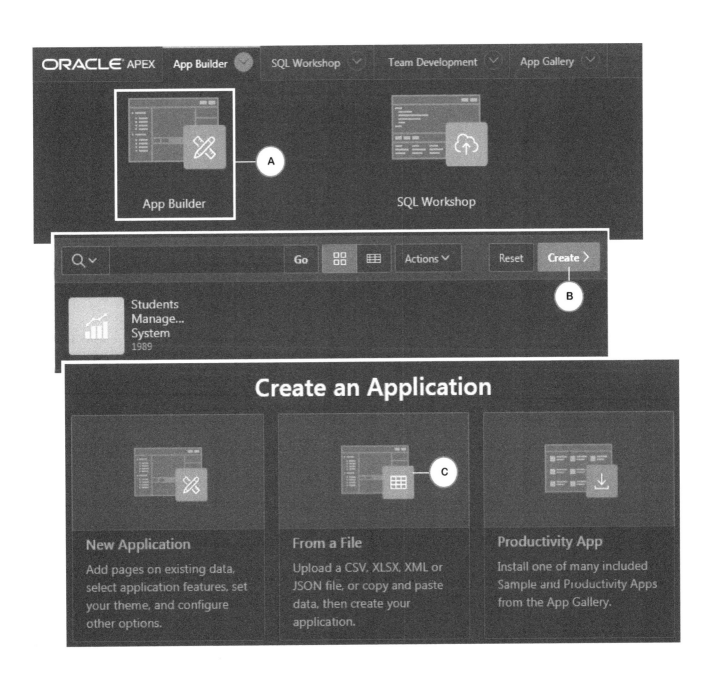

STEP

2

On the Load Data page, select the **Upload a File** tab (A). Click the **Choose File** button (B), and select the MS Excel file (**books.xlsx**) from your computer. Alternatively, you can drag and drop the file in the marked rectangle area. The uploading status (C) will be displayed at the bottom of your screen during the process.

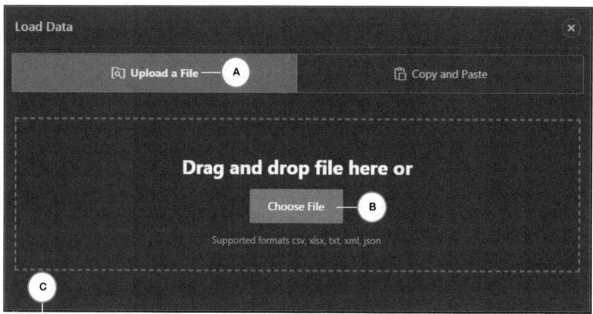

STEP

3

After uploading data from the data file, another screen will pop up asking for data destination. On this screen, select the **New Table** option (A) to put the uploaded data into a new database table. Enter **BOOKS** (B) in the Table Name box, and click the **Load Data** button (C). This screen has several other options that are not currently related to our scenario. After processing the file, you will get a confirmation (D) informing that the new BOOKS table is created with 30 rows. Click the **Create Application** button (E).

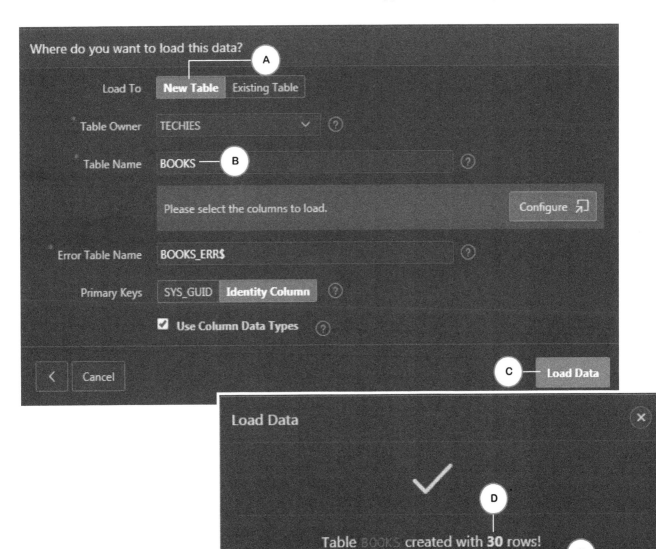

STEP

4

On this occasion, APEX will create the following additional pages (A). The Home page will display four cards to access the other four pages. The Dashboard page will display some bar charts. The Book Search page is a Faceted Search page. The Books Report page is an interactive report page. The Calendar page will provide publication date information in a calendar. Click the **Edit** icon (B) next to the Faceted Search page. On the ensuing page, select the **Cards** option (C) to see data in cards. Set Card Title to **TITLE** (D), Description Column to **IMAGE_PATH** (E), and Additional Text Column to **GENRE** (F). The three values you selected are columns in the BOOKS table. Click the **Save Changes** button (G), followed by the **Create Application** button (H).

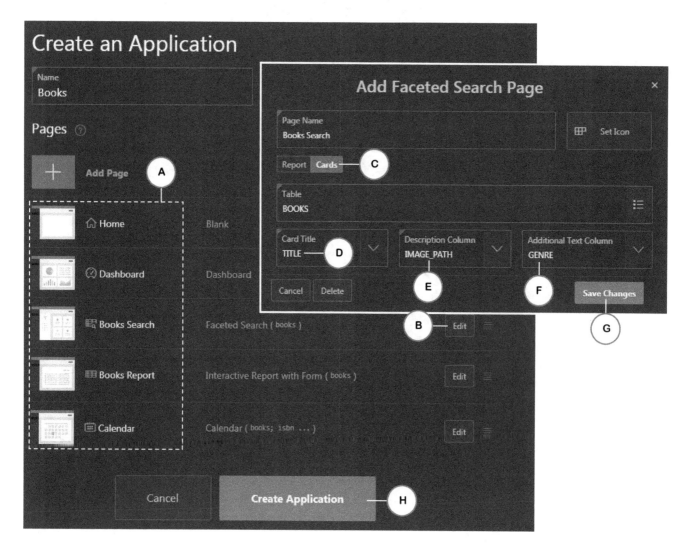

This the Home page of your new application, which contains four cards. In addition to the main menu, you can use these cards to access relevant pages.

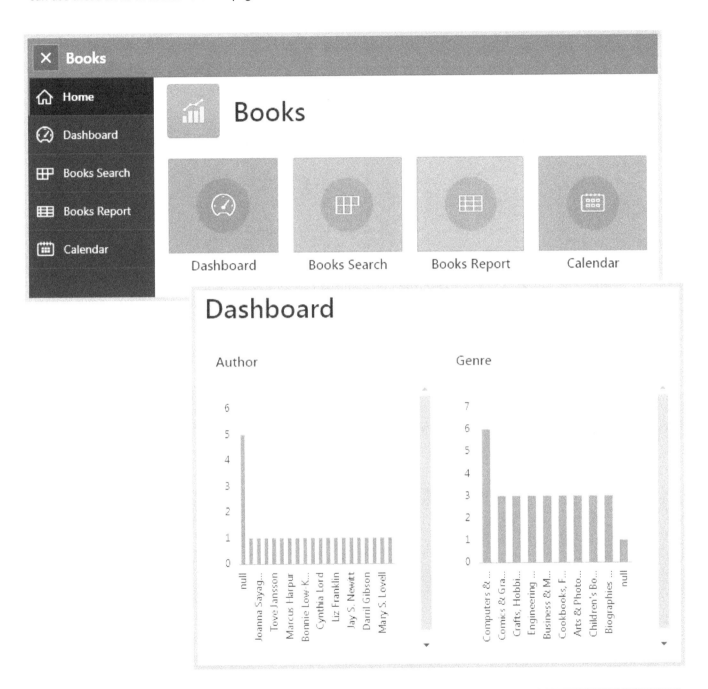

The Dashboard page comprises some auto-generated charts based on the BOOKS table data.

The Books Search page is a Faceted Search page. Faceted Search feature was introduced in APEX 19.2. This feature allows you to set filters using Facets (A) that usually appear on the left side of the screen. A facet shows possible values together with the occurrence count (B) within the result set. After the end user changed a facet, results, dependent facets and occurrence counts refresh immediately – the results in the current scenario are shown in cards (C). Using the Search box (D) you can find something instantly. For example, type analysis and press Enter. You will see a book titled Geographic Information Analysis. Remove the word analysis from the search box to make it empty and press Enter. The filter will be removed and all books will re-appear on the screen.

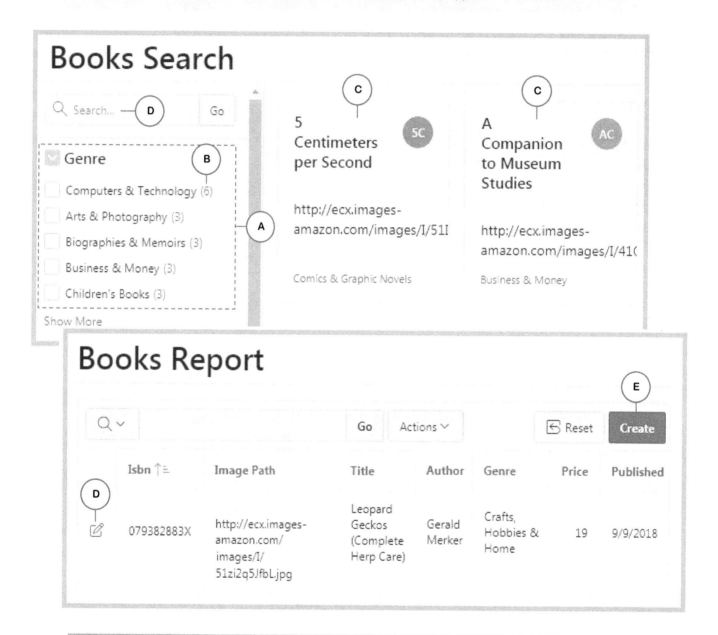

The Books Report module comprises the conventional interactive report and input form pages that you have already seen in the previous chapter. You can modify a book record using the edit icon (D), and can also add new books through the Create button (E). In this chapter, however, we will try to explore some more interesting things about interactive report.

The Calendar page is the last auto-generated page of our application, which displays books information by publication date. The calendar page is usually added to applications to render events. It allows you to create drill-down links to information stored in specific columns and enable drag and drop capability. In our application, this page is generated by the app builder because we have a date type column (PUBLISHED) in the BOOKS table. A calendar is created with monthly, daily, and list views. The Previous and Next buttons (A) are used to switch back and forth in the calendar.

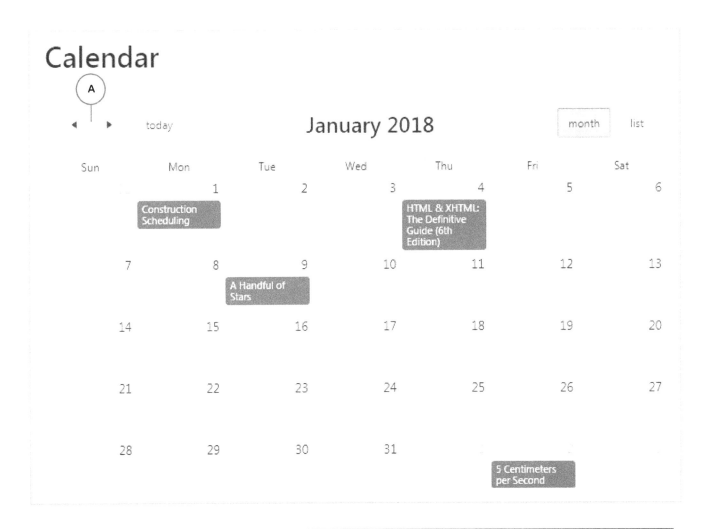

In our scenario, the calendar will show books information by publication date in respective date cells. For example, the Construction Scheduling book was published on 1st January 2018, so it appears in the corresponding date cell. Right now, the calendar will be displaying ISBN instead of book titles on your screen. You will make this change in a subsequent exercise.

5.2 The Home Page

As you know, Oracle APEX app creation wizard creates Login and Home pages for every application. In contrast to the previous app, the Home page in this app is not blank. It is created with four navigational cards – Dashboard, Book Search, Book Report, and Calendar. In this section I'll provide some briefs about the Home page of this application.

If you click the Quick Edit option (A) in the Developer Toolbar and move your mouse pointer over the four cards on the Home page, you will see a rectangle border (B) around the card region. Click any card. This action will switch you to the Page Designer tab in your browser. On the Rendering tab, click Page Navigation region (C). In the Property Editor, click the Go to List icon (D). Click Edit Component (E). You will be taken to the List Details page in Shared Components, where you will see four entries (F) auto-generated by APEX. The four cards being displayed on the Home page are using these list entries for navigation.

Click the Dashboard entry link (G). On the Create/Edit page, have a look at the Page attribute in the Target section (H). The value 2 in this attribute is the target page in the application that is invoked when you click the Dashboard card on the Home page. Click the Cancel button and switch back to Page Designer. Click the Attributes node (I). The List Template property is set to Cards (J) to displays the Page Navigation list as cards. Click Template Options (K), and try the other options provided for the Cards template. After selecting these options, save the changes and then run the page using the Save and Run page button.

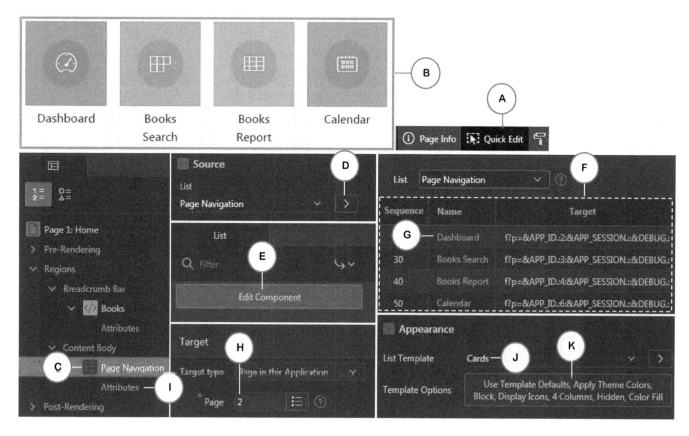

5.3 The Dashboard Page

The dashboard page created by the App Builder contains some bar charts that are based on the BOOKS table. In this section you will learn how to tweak these bar charts and convert them into pie charts to get some insight into books information.

The Author chart is meant to display number of books written by each author. By default, App Builder created this as a bar chart. You will transform it into a pie chart.

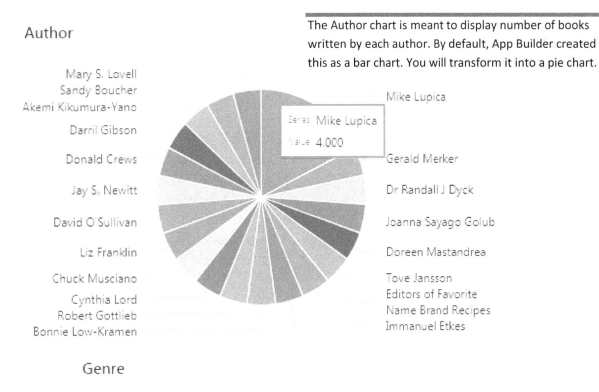

The Genre chart will also be transformed into a pie chart to show number of books under each genre.

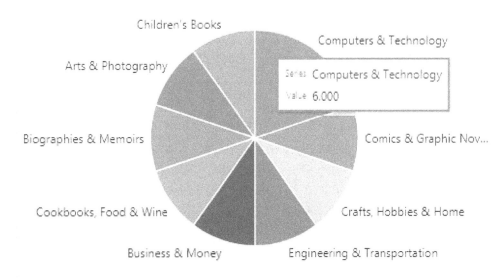

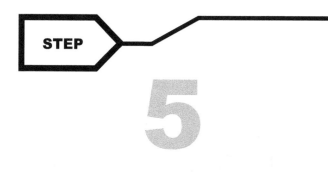

STEP 5

Open Page 2 (Dashboard) in Page Designer using the arrow keys (A). Click the **Author** chart region (B). The Type of this region in the Property Editor will show Chart (C), meaning that this is a chart type region. Click **Attributes** (D), and change the Type of this chart from Bar to **Pie** (E). Click **Series 1** (F), and have a look at the SQL Query (G) in the Property Editor. If you are familiar with SQL language, then you can easily follow what this

SELECT statement is doing. It is powering the chart by grabbing number of books written by each author. Scroll down a bit and see the Link section (H). Each slice in the pie chart acts as a link via the values set in this section. When you click a slice, you are redirected to Page 4 (Books Report) using the value Page 4 (I) set in the Target property. A filter (J) is set in the Target property, which displays books information of the selected author. Scroll down a bit to the Label section. Turn on the **Show** option (K). Set label Position to **Outside Slice** and Display As to **Label** to show authors' names outside the pie chart slices. Save and run the page. In the Author pie chart, as illustrated on the previous page, Mike Lupica's slice is bigger than other authors, because he has authored more books. Click this slice and see details of this author on Page 4.

STEP

6

Expand the **Genre** region (A). The Type of this region is also set to Chart (D). Click **Attributes** (B), and change the Type of this chart from Bar to **Pie** (E). Click **Series 1** (C), and view the SQL Query for this chart. The only difference between the previous one and this query is the GENRE column (F). Each slice in this pie chart also acts as a link. When you click a slice, you are redirected to Page 4 (G) (Books Report). Click the Page 4 link (G) to see a filter (H) in the Target dialog, which will display books information of the selected genre. Finally, set properties in the Label section (I). Save and run the page. In the Genre pie chart, Computer & Technology genre's slice is bigger than others. Click this slice and see details of this genre on Page 4.

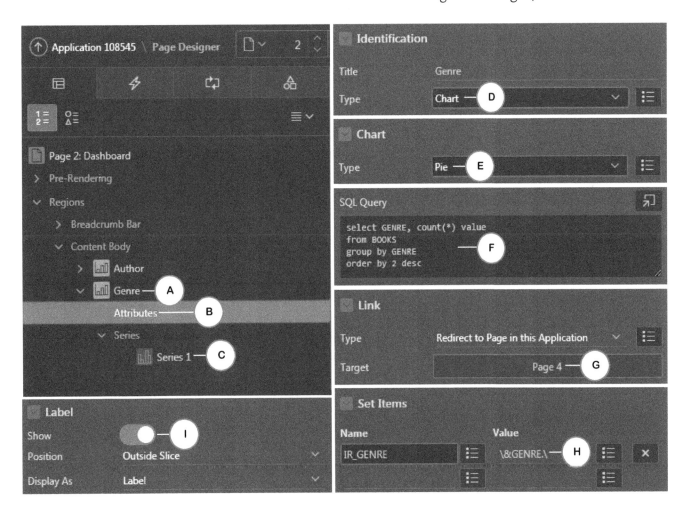

5.4 The Books Report Page

The Books Report page contains an interactive report showing information from the BOOKS table. You have already used and went through auto-generated features and functionalities of interactive report in the previous chapter. You can use this page to add, modify, and delete books' information as well.

The focus of this section is to introduce some other options like Chart, Group by and Pivot (A) in the Actions menu that were skipped in the previous chapter. If you click a column's heading (for example, Image Path), a menu (B) appears on your screen with four options – Sort Ascending, Sort Descending, Hide Column, and Control Break. If you want to hide a column, click the Hide Column option (C). After hiding the column you have to save the report. You can bring it back using the Columns option (D) in the Actions menu.

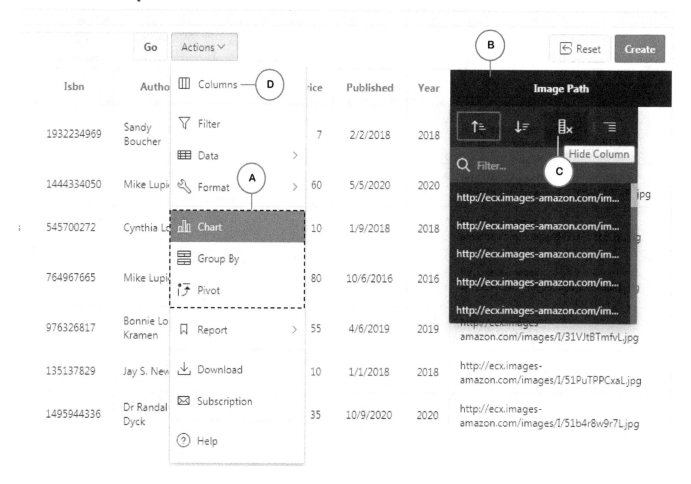

STEP

7

CHART VIEW

Let's create a chart to view number of books in each genre. From the Actions menu choose the **Chart** option. The Chart dialog box (A) will appear. In this dialog box, keep the default **Bar** chart tab (B) selected. For Label, select **Genre** (C). From the Function list, choose **Count** (D). Click the **Apply** button (E). This action will add a View Chart icon (F) to the interactive report. Click this icon to view the chart (G) you just added. To view the default interactive report, click the View Report icon (H). To modify the chart's parameter, click the Edit Chart link (I). As you can see the Computer & Technology genre (J) has six books, hence its bar is taller than other genres. Save the chart by selecting Actions menu | Report | Save Report. In the Save Report dialog, select **As Default Report Settings** from the Save list. Then, select the **Primary** option and click **Apply**.

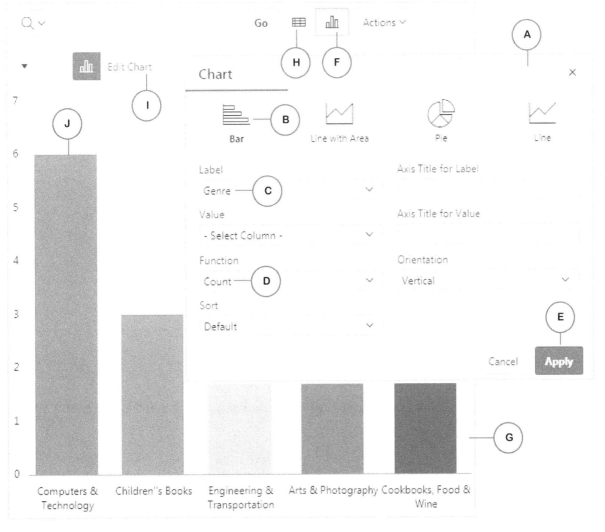

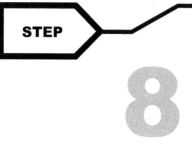

STEP

8

Next, we are going to test the Group by option. When you click this option in the Actions menu, the Group By dialog box (A) pops up. From the first list, select the **Author** column (B) to group all records in the BOOKS table by this column. From the Functions list, select **Count** (C) to count number of books written by each author. Enter **No. of Books** (D) in the Label box. A calculated column with this label (E) will be created to display number of books written by each author. Also, turn on the Sum option (F) to display a grand total (G) at the bottom. Click **Apply** (H). A summarized view from the BOOKS table (I) will appear on your screen, along with a new icon labeled View Group By (J). The Group By view will be displayed when this icon is current. Click the **No. of Books** column's heading (E) and sort the view as indicated in point (K). **Save** this view by following the previous instructions.

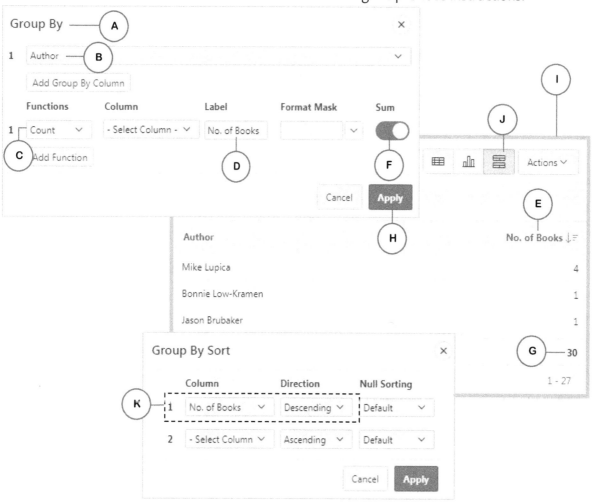

STEP

9

In this step you will create a Pivot table. The Pivot option is the Actions menu is used to create a cross tab view based on the data in the main interactive report. Click the **View Report** icon. Click **Pivot** in the Actions menu. In the Pivot dialog screen (A), select **Year** for Pivot Columns (B) to display the Year column's data across the screen (C). Select **Genre** (D) for Row Columns to display genre data in rows (E). Select **Count** function (F). Enter **Published** for Label (G). Turn on the **Sum** option (H) to show grand totals (I) for each year. Click **Apply** (J). The output of your selections yields a pivot table with a View Pivot icon (K), to shows number of books published in each year from 2016 to 2020. Save your work. Edit the pivot table, interchange the Year and Genre columns and observe the change.

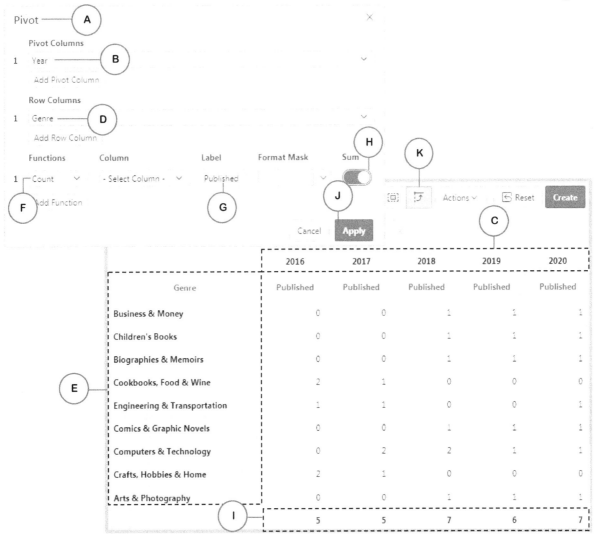

Genre	2016 Published	2017 Published	2018 Published	2019 Published	2020 Published
Business & Money	0	0	1	1	1
Children's Books	0	0	1	1	1
Biographies & Memoirs	0	0	1	1	1
Cookbooks, Food & Wine	2	1	0	0	0
Engineering & Transportation	1	1	0	0	1
Comics & Graphic Novels	0	0	1	1	1
Computers & Technology	0	2	2	1	1
Crafts, Hobbies & Home	2	1	0	0	0
Arts & Photography	0	0	1	1	1
	5	5	7	6	7

5.5 The Books Search Page

The Books Search page is auto-generated with Faceted Search feature. It contains two panes. The left pane contains a search box and multiple facets that you can use to set filters, while the right pane displays books information.

The default view of this page is different from the one illustrated here. In this section, you will set a few properties to give it the following look. If you select Computers & Technology in the Genre facet, you'll see six books from this genre in the right pane. With this selection, the Price and Author facets are also updated to display relevant price and author information. Click the Clear link (A) to clear the applied filter(s). Type business in the search box (B), and click Go (C) to see books from Business & Money genre.

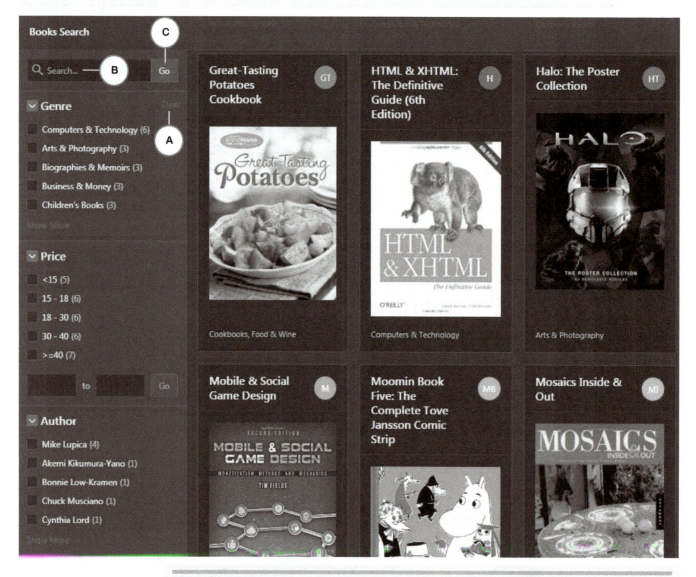

The right pane displays information from the BOOKS table. You will use IMAGE_PATH column in the BOOKS table to display images from Amazon's site. These images will act as links. When you click an image, you are redirected to Amazon's site to see details of the selected book.

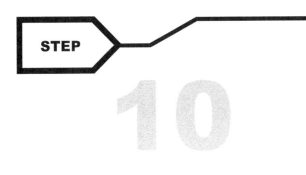

STEP

From the main application menu, select **Books Search**. Click the **Edit Page** link in the Developer Toolbar to open it in Page Designer. Expand the Columns node under the Books region, and click **CARD_TEXT** (A). In the Property Editor, add image markup (B) in HTML Expression property.

The img HTML tag displays images of books using the IMAGE_PATH column data. Click **Attributes** (C) and then click **Template Options** (D) in Property Editor. In Template Options dialog, select **5 Columns** (E) from the Layout list to display 5 books on each row. Click **OK**. Click the Books region (F). Alter the default SQL Query by prefixing a URL (G) (Amazon's web address) to the CARD_LINK column. The link will take you to Amazon's site to get details of books. The markup and CARD_LINK URL are available in Markup.txt file provided with the book source. **Save** and run the page. Play around with facets and click images of books to see details on Amazon's site.

5.6 The Calendar Page

By default, the application displays ISBN of books in calendar cells. In this step you will display titles of books in calendar cells instead of ISBN.

STEP

11

In the application menu, click the **Calendar** option. Using the previous button (A) switch back to January 2018. Click the **Edit Page** link (B) in the Developer Toolbar to access the source of this page. In Page Designer, click the Attributes node (C) under the Calendar region. In the Property Editor pane, change Display Column from ISBN to **TITLE**. Save and run the page. It should now display titles of books, as illustrated in the following figure. Rest your mouse pointer on book titles to see their publication dates.

5.7 Change Application Style

In this final step, you will change the default style of your application. In addition to the default Vista style, you have three more options – Vita-Dark, Vita-Red, and Vita-Slate.

STEP

12

In the Developer toolbar, click Theme Roller (A). In the Theme Roller screen, select **Vita – Dark** (B) from the Style list, and click **Set as Current** (C) to set this style for your application. Click **OK** in the confirmation box and close the Theme Roller screen (D). Now the page will resemble the figure illustrated on the next page. Access other pages of the application to see the newly applied style.

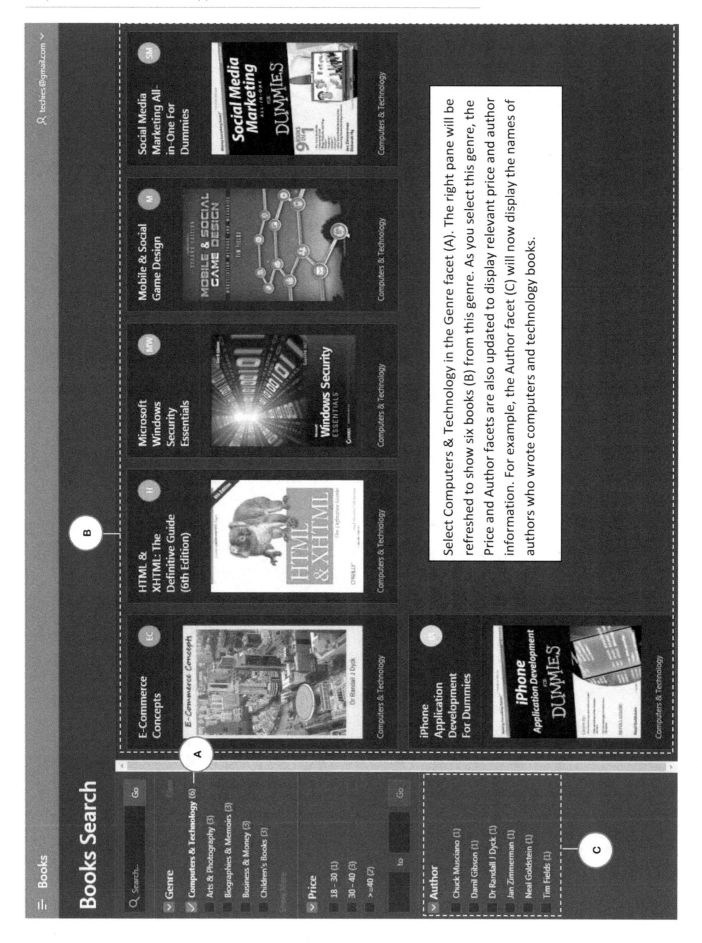

Select Computers & Technology in the Genre facet (A). The right pane will be refreshed to show six books (B) from this genre. As you select this genre, the Price and Author facets are also updated to display relevant price and author information. For example, the Author facet (C) will now display the names of authors who wrote computers and technology books.

Conclusion

This book by no means is a complete introduction to Oracle APEX. In this compact guide I just tried to draw you into the exciting world of web application development. If I succeeded to ignite your desire to become a professional web developer, then I encourage you to read my next-level book – Oracle APEX 20 For Beginners (ISBN: 979-8633931839). To become a serious Oracle APEX developer you have to have some knowledge of SQL and PL/SQL. I know that most of you may not be familiar with these languages. So, to help you out I'm providing my SQL/PLSQL e-book for free. Please email me the purchase proof of this book at oratech@cyber.net.pk to get the free e-book. Go through the e-book, get grips on SQL and PLSQL, then grab a copy of my afore-mentioned book to learn some next-level stuff.

I'm very much grateful to you for taking the time to read this book. I spent a lot of time to compile the exercises in this book and to make them as simple as possible. I hope that you enjoyed reading them, as much as I have enjoyed writing them. If I can give you one last piece of advice, it's to always keep learning and don't give up. With hard work and effort, you can accomplish anything.

Good Luck!

Index